"Stephanie Kriesberg has written a reassuring and easy-to-read book about what it's like to grow up with a mother who is raising you to meet her own needs and is generally incapable of empathy. Kriesberg describes the causes of narcissism in vivid prose. Replete with real-life examples, exercises, and thoughtful journaling questions, I will be sending clients and friends to this book again and again."

—**Jonice Webb, PhD**, psychologist,
and author of *Running On Empty*
and *Running On Empty No More*

"Stephanie has neatly captured the multitude of ways in which having a narcissistic parent can constrain your own development and cause turmoil in family functioning whilst also acknowledging the different forms of narcissism, each with their unique behavioral repertoires. Narcissists resist change; however, this is an excellent resource for developing skills for dealing with your narcissistic mother—for you and your (future) family."

—**Claire M. Hart, PhD**, narcissism researcher
and associate professor of psychology at
the University of Southampton, UK

"Stephanie Kriesberg's book fills an important need for women trying to understand and heal from the myriad issues resulting from being raised by a narcissistic mother. Kriesberg skillfully weaves together a number of treatment modalities to provide practical strategies for coping and recovery. This is a beautifully written and very accessible self-help book. I will definitely recommend it to my clients who come from this kind of background."

—**Lorna McKenzie-Pollock, LICSW**, director of education
for the New England Society of Clinical Hypnosis;
with a private practice in Brookline, MA

"An intricate and eye-opening dive into maternal narcissism. Through a series of compelling vignettes and applied exercises, Kriesberg provides the perfect road map for understanding, navigating, and overcoming the impacts of being raised by a narcissistic mother. Highly recommend!"

—**Jill A. Stoddard, PhD**, author of *Be Mighty*
and *The Big Book of ACT Metaphors*

"Filled with dozens of relatable stories and curative coping tools, Kriesberg's guide is like having a compassionate therapist in your pocket who shows you how to navigate the conflicting feelings of dealing with a self-centered mother so you can confidently set boundaries, honor your own needs, and put yourself back in the center of your own life."

—**Courtney Armstrong, LPC**, author of *Rethinking Trauma Treatment*

"Women struggling with the emotional impoverishment and instability of life with a narcissistic mother will find themselves on long-sought solid ground with Stephanie Kriesberg's *Adult Daughters of Narcissistic Mothers*. Straightforward, reassuring, and interactive, this welcome guide provides an admirable balance of relatable examples, compassionate validation, and proven strategies for healing."

—**Julie L. Hall**, founder of The Narcissist Family Files,
and author of *The Narcissist in Your Life*

"This is a hands-on, straight-to-the-point, useful guide for processing challenging residual experiences of mothers exposing a narcissistic personality. Facing the range from distant ignorance to intrusive preoccupation—all in the service of the mother's own self-interest—has a major impact on a daughter's continuing internal sense of self. The author connects close descriptions of internal struggle with systematic and thoughtful strategies for daughters' healing and growth."

—**Elsa Ronningstam, PhD**, associate professor (PT) at Harvard
Medical School, and clinical psychologist at McLean Hospital

Adult Daughters of Narcissistic Mothers

quiet the critical voice in your head,
heal self-doubt, *and*
live the life you deserve

Stephanie M. Kriesberg, PsyD

New Harbinger Publications, Inc.

Publisher's Note

NEW HARBINGER PUBLICATIONS is a registered trademark of New Harbinger Publications, Inc.

New Harbinger Publications is an employee-owned company.

Copyright © 2022 by Stephanie Kriesberg
New Harbinger Publications, Inc.
5674 Shattuck Avenue
Oakland, CA 94609
www.newharbinger.com

All Rights Reserved

Cover design by Amy Daniel

Acquired by Georgia Kolias

Edited by Gretel Hakanson

Library of Congress Cataloging-in-Publication Data

Names: Kriesberg, Stephanie M., author.
Title: Adult daughters of narcissistic mothers : quiet the critical voice in your head, heal
    self-doubt, and live the life you deserve / Stephanie M. Kriesberg, PsyD.
Description: Oakland, CA : New Harbinger Publications, [2022] | Includes bibliographi-
    cal references.
Identifiers: LCCN 2022020012 | ISBN 9781648480096 (trade paperback)
Subjects: LCSH: Narcissism. | Self-acceptance. | Mothers and daughters--Psychology. |
    BISAC: FAMILY & RELATIONSHIPS / Parenting / Parent & Adult Child |
    SELF-HELP / Emotions
Classification: LCC BF575.N35 K75 2022 | DDC 155.2--dc23/eng/20220709
LC record available at https://lccn.loc.gov/2022020012

Printed in the United States of America

24   23   22

10   9   8   7   6   5   4   3   2   1   First Printing

*For Ellis
and for Lea and Talia
with love*

Contents

Foreword   vii

Introduction   1

Chapter 1   Being the Daughter of a Narcissist Mother   7

Chapter 2   Understanding Your Mother   23

Chapter 3   Is She a Grandiose or Vulnerable Narcissist?   41

Chapter 4   Identifying Gaslighting and Lack of Empathy   55

Chapter 5   Disrupt Your Anxious Thought Patterns   71

Chapter 6   Release Your Shame and Grief   85

Chapter 7   Soothe Your Emotional Roller Coaster   101

Chapter 8   Find Your Core Strengths and Build Confidence   115

Chapter 9   Building Boundaries and Becoming Assertive   129

Chapter 10   Relationships and Creating Your Life   145

Parting Words   159

Acknowledgments   161

References   163

Foreword

With the widespread use of the term "narcissism" in recent years, many have come to imagine and perhaps even identify issues of narcissism in their own personal relationships, past and present. What's harder to fathom, apart from movies like *Mommie Dearest, Gypsy,* and *Ordinary People,* is the reality of a narcissistic mother. We tend to count on maternal instinct to foster a needs-meeting inclination—one that will protect, nurture, support, guide, and cherish the helpless and precious child. But this is simply not the case for every person residing in the privileged and important role of "mom."

In my work treating narcissistic people and those offended by the narcissist, it is not uncommon for me to meet someone who has been plagued by early embedded messages of unlovability, inadequacy, and undesirability—the internalized voice of a devaluing, demanding, and dismissive narcissistic parent. The silencing of one's voice juxtaposed with deafening self-doubt, subjugation, and self-sacrifice become representations on the emotional blueprint designed for present and future coping and survival.

The narcissistic parent can cast a devastating shadow on the self-esteem of her young ones. In some cases, the child is destined to forever be toting the heavy spotlight upon their shoulders, casting its glow on the parent's insatiable ego. This *hefty spotlight* might be seen as the little girl who always must be in perfect sync with her narcissistic mom's wishes and vicarious unfulfilled dreams, to validate and support Mom in achieving the (requisite) enviable extraordinary, best performance, in the eyes of others…even if only imagined.

Therefore, I could not be more delighted to endorse Stephanie Kriesberg's beautifully written book, *Adult Daughters of Narcissistic Mothers.* Hats off to Stephanie for this valuable endeavor. Crafted through a clear, personal, and thoughtful voice, her book offers the reader the highly effective skills and tools needed to overcome the anxiety, self-blame, shame, and self-doubt that come from having a self-absorbed, narcissistic mother. Readers will learn skills for developing their core strengths, setting limits, and regulating the painful emotions arising from the haunting triggers of remembered experiences and longstanding unchallenged responses. She teaches the reader how to "trust your inner advocate" and become free from the control of a narcissistic mother, breaking the legacy of learned negative messages that cause anxiety, self-doubt, and worry.

The author, in personal and practical language, outlines the strategies for cultivating a keen internal compass—one that allows for both mindful awareness of the internal struggle as well as tools for bypassing self-defeating patterns in favor of healthy ones. Anyone who has been raised by a narcissistic mother will surely resonate with the vivid precision of Stephanie's descriptions and vignettes.

If you or someone you know has suffered the challenges of dealing with a narcissistic mother, the "truths" that linger and sting the heart, the painful burdens of ongoing intrusive engagements with the narcissist, I thoroughly and confidently recommend you read this book and add it to your resource library. Dr. Kriesberg has dedicated many years to her clinical expertise in this area, and in this heartfelt and instrumental book, she generously gifts the reader with a thoughtful guide for engaging healing, liberation from invisibility and low self-worth, and effective strategies for living the healthy life you truly deserve!

—Wendy T. Behary

Author of the internationally bestselling book *Disarming the Narcissist*

Introduction

What made you pick up this book? You long to feel better. You've had enough of feeling different from other women. Maybe you've accomplished a lot in your life; maybe you haven't gotten there yet. Either way, it feels as if no one knows the real you, the one you keep hidden, perhaps even from yourself. No one knows how you feel stuck in self-doubt. No one hears the voice criticizing you in your mind, like a blaring car alarm with no off button. So often you feel alone inside, even when you're with other people, because no one really understands how you feel or why. Perhaps you don't understand your feelings either exactly.

You've tried hard to do everything right, maybe to be as perfect as you can. But no matter what, you feel you're missing the mark. As for asking for help? Forget about it. You need to do things on your own. Anyway, it's hard to reach out when you don't know what you want or how you feel. It's like living in a bubble. But part of you can sense there's life outside that bubble, and you want out.

Maybe you're holding this book because there was one last straw that broke your emotional camel's back. Perhaps you were standing in the supermarket, picking out a Mother's Day card, feeling sad or resentful, as you read the flowery tributes that sound nothing like your feelings about your mother. Perhaps you're tired of dreading your mother's phone calls and how bad you feel about yourself afterward. Perhaps a friend or loved one suggested: "I think your mother might be narcissistic." Maybe it's just wanting out of that bubble. So you hit the internet or went to the book-store and found something that sounded familiar. And here you are.

Do You Have a Narcissistic Mother?

What's it like to have a narcissistic mother? *Narcissism* is a term that's talked about frequently in the media. However, you probably want to know: How does narcissism show up in mothers, and how does it impact daughters, like you, throughout their lives? Since you picked up this book, your mother may demonstrate the following traits, among others:

- Lack of empathy or hit-or-miss, roller-coaster empathy

- Constant self-focus

- Emotional immaturity, as if she's a child or preteen in an adult's body

- Difficulty having true close relationships

- Black-and-white thinking

- Inflexible, rigid approach to life

- Explosive emotions

As her daughter, you may struggle with:

- Self-criticism that's like a tape constantly playing in your head

- Worrying about the future

- Obsessing about the past

- Feeling inadequate

- Self-blame

- Isolating yourself

- Holding yourself back from opportunities, relationships, friendships, fun

Sound familiar? The good news is that you can find relief from these problems and learn skills to develop calm and confidence. This book is based on my career as a clinical psychologist working with daughters of narcissistic mothers. I've worked with many women like you who have found their way out of their bubbles.

Many women seek help when they reach a milestone in their lives: graduating from college, getting married, having a baby, placing an elderly mother in a nursing home. These turning points can create stressful moments for everyone. However, when you're dealing with a narcissistic mother, you get more than stressful moments. You often find that your joy or need for support is overshadowed by a mother's needs or behavior.

Other daughters come to therapy in the midst of everyday life: going to school, working, planning a family vacation. Even if your mother is not alive or you have no or little contact with her, you may hear her voice in your head. The critical, unkind voice may now be your own. That inner voice is so loud, takes up so much airtime in your mind, and has so much power over how you see yourself and your relationships.

You're Not Alone

One of the most painful aspects of your experience may be feeling ashamed about your difficult relationship with your mother, on top of feeling bad about yourself. The whole mess of feelings is kept inside, not discussed or revealed. Who would understand? As one woman told me: "We're like a secret society." But keeping secrets is painful and increases feelings of shame and anxiety. That's where this book can help.

I'll pull back the curtain on this secret society. This book has several purposes, including helping you realize that you're not alone and that your emotions and experiences are shared by many women. Unfortunately, we can't say exactly how many women have narcissistic mothers. Approximately 4.8 percent of American females meet the criteria for narcissistic personality disorder (Stinson et al. 2008). Since there are 158 million females in the United States, we can speculate that there are about 7.6 million narcissistic females (US Department of Health and Human Services 2013). That's a large number of women potentially raising daughters. In addition, narcissism is a spectrum disorder (Malkin 2015). As such, many more women may have significant narcissistic traits that impact their daughters. Throughout this book, I'll share stories of women like you, in the form of composites to protect the confidentiality of the women with whom I've worked. I'll share the journeys they've taken and the skills they have learned to find their authentic selves and to hear, and listen to, their inner voices.

How This Book Can Help You

This book has several specific goals. By the end of this book, you'll have a toolbox of knowledge and skills to handle the anxiety, self-blame, shame, and self-doubt that can emerge from having a mother with narcissistic traits. A primary goal is for you to discover who you are and what you want, so you can break the psychological grip that your mother holds on you. This means finding the self-confidence to hear and to trust your inner voice. That might seem impossible right now. But it isn't. I have seen it happen for many women who practice the steps in this book. It can happen for you too.

This book weaves together skills from several areas of psychology because research shows this is a highly effective approach for treating mental health issues, especially anxiety (Daitch 2018). Below is brief explanation of each and why I chose them.

Acceptance and commitment therapy (ACT) teaches that we can't help what shows up inside us—our thoughts, emotions, physical sensations, urges, and memories (called private events in ACT). You may feel that your thoughts and feelings about your relationships with your mother rule your life. Then you feel bad for having those thoughts and feelings! ACT guides you to be aware of your private events in the here and now and to make space for them. ACT helps you understand what really matters to you (called "values" in ACT) and to take active steps to create that life. Ultimately, the purpose of ACT is to help you become psychologically flexible. That means being willing to come into contact with all your experiences, whether painful or not, and take actions based on what is important to you (Gordon and Boroshuk 2017).

Cognitive behavior therapy (CBT) helps you identify unhelpful thinking and behavior patterns and learn different skills to handle them.

Mindful self-compassion therapy (MSC) teaches you to be as kind and compassionate toward yourself as you are toward others. This helps with the harsh and self-critical voice playing in your head.

Solution-focused brief therapy (SFBT) is based on the idea that you hold the solutions to your problems within yourself. Through examining the ways in which you've handled life's challenges, you'll find the confidence and self-awareness to handle challenges with your mother and other areas of your life.

Mindfulness means developing your ability to pay attention to what's happening in the here and now, without judging your experience or yourself. It's important to note that you don't have to meditate to practice mindfulness, although you can if you want to. You can practice mindfulness as you do day-to-day activities, such as drinking your coffee or brushing your teeth.

Guided visualization helps people with a broad range of issues from preparing for surgery or giving a speech to grieving a loss. Research demonstrates that rehearsing something in our minds can be just as effective as rehearsing something in real life. Guided visualization helps you develop relaxation skills, rehearse challenging life situations, and review past successes (Armstrong, 2015).

This book is full of practices that encourage you to write down your reactions, thoughts, and feelings. Memories and emotional reactions will likely emerge naturally as you read. I recommend you have a notebook or journal dedicated for this book. If you prefer to write on a device such as your phone, that's okay too. In addition, worksheets and recordings of the meditations and guided visualizations are offered on the website for this book at http://www.newharbinger.com/50096, and you can listen to them on your phone, computer, or tablet. Remember, the main purpose is for you to find your own voice. That starts with figuring out how to use this book in the way that's right for you.

This book is meant to help daughters of narcissistic mothers understand themselves and their pain and learn ways to thrive as fully as possible. I also encourage understanding and treating narcissistic mothers with empathy, dignity, and compassion. Nobody wants to be a narcissistic mother. It is undoubtedly an unsatisfying way to live. In addition, we live in a culture that either glorifies mothers (those Mother's Day cards) or vilifies them (think nagging sitcom moms). As a mother of two daughters myself, I have been humbled by the difficulty of the job and how easy it is to make mistakes. That being said, my wish for you is that understanding will help *you* heal. Therefore, this book is *not* a prescription for your behavior toward your mother, and it is certainly *not* a demand for you to forgive and forget. Only you can decide what is right for you in terms of your emotions and your relationship with your mother.

I'd like to say that by the time you finish reading this book, you'll no longer have any painful feelings about your mother. I'd like to say you that you'll be free of self-critical thoughts forever. No more knots in your stomach. No more wanting to hide from or slam the phone down on your mother. No remembering the painful comment from your high school graduation. But I can't. As human beings, we're simply not wired that way.

As much as we'd like to, we can't control the thoughts and emotions that show up inside us. We can't control when our body reacts in fear, with our palms sweating and our hearts pounding. We can't control the desire to do something impulsive, like send an angry email. We can only control our own actions. We can't control our human tendency to want to avoid uncomfortable feelings in all the ways modern humans have devised, such as working too many hours or focusing on our phones. But we can learn to listen to our own voice, separate from our mother's, and live life on our own terms.

No matter their age, their stage in life, or even if their mother is not alive, I hear daughters of narcissistic mother wanting the same thing: freedom inside their own minds. I hear them longing to wake up in the morning hearing their own voice instead of their mother's. They want to feel separate. They want to know that they are their own people, making their own choices and living the lives they want. You can have that. Let's get started.

Chapter 1

Being the Daughter of a
Narcissist Mother

Do you feel that no matter how hard you try, you can't get rid of feeling sad, angry, or bad about yourself? Maybe you'd like to feel as other women seem to, talking about their emotions and their friendship-filled lives. Perhaps you'd like to state your opinions without worrying that no one will care or that you'll be rejected if someone doesn't like what you say. But you keep quiet. Or maybe you have no problem speaking up. You blurt things out, then feel guilty and frustrated, which isn't good for your relationships or your self-esteem. But when you feel anxious or angry, you get so overwhelmed, you can't stop yourself. Let's add that you're tired of feeling guilty all the time for making your own choices: about where to live, your profession, your identity, or how you spend your time. It's no wonder others don't see or know you, even if you're right there with them.

I suspect that you're reading this book because you've started to figure out there is a connection between your relationship with your mother and how you feel and function. As such, you may long for your mother's approval. Perhaps you constantly hear your mother's voice in your head, criticizing you. It's an endless recording, as you mentally review past conversations or arguments with your mother, berating yourself for speaking up or staying silent. Maybe you focus on the future, worried about Mom's next complaint or demand. Or you do both, your mind toggling back and forth between past and present mother-related anxieties. You may also feel that you're trying to mourn the relationship with your mother, the one you never had, even if she's still alive.

As adults, some women want to see their mothers less frequently because those interactions leave them feeling angry, depressed, even "crazy." Every day daughters of narcissistic mothers agonize over questions such as: Do I have to invite Mom to Thanksgiving? Should I block her number? Is it safe to let her spend time with my children? How will I deal with Mother's Day?

A part of you may want to end the relationship completely, but the idea is terrifying. What kind of daughter does that? She's getting old. You want to be a good person. Who will take care of her? What about your children—do they deserve to know their grandmother, even if she causes you so much pain? And what will happen to your relationships with the rest of the family if you don't see her anymore? No wonder you feel overwhelmed, depleted, stuck. It's not easy to answer these questions. It can feel like entering a dark tunnel, and there's no way out. No matter your goal or stage in life, what you need is a healthy relationship with yourself, one in which you can hear your own voice clearly and authentically. That is the primary goal of this book: to feel untangled, separate, and seen.

How Did You Get This Way?

In the next chapter, you'll learn in detail about the psychological makeup of narcissistic mothers. For now, it's important to know that you probably experienced some, or all, of the following when you were growing up. In families with a narcissistic mother, things are upside down. In a healthy family, the children's needs come first. The parents, as best they can, take care of the children. However, a narcissistic parent is unable to do that, at least not consistently enough. Instead, the parent's needs and feelings are most important. Children with narcissistic mothers learn to squash down their own feelings. They "read" those of their mothers, like human radar detectors. A child's struggles or needs are problems to the family, not problems to be understood and solved with compassion (Donaldson-Pressman 1994).

Think of the family with a narcissistic parent like this: It's like a container that's been stuffed with too many plants. There's soil, and the plants are watered and given sunlight and maybe plant food. But there are just too many plants in the container for them to thrive. All the plants are grabbing for nutrients from the soil. There's not enough for all of them to grow and be healthy. Let's look at Holly's story and her struggles as the daughter of a narcissistic mother. Later in the book, we'll look at how she broke free and found her "space" in life.

Holly, age forty-five, is a real estate agent with curly hair and a warm smile that puts her clients at ease. She races from her last showing to her twelve-year-old daughter Sophie's soccer game. Even with her GPS, it's tricky to find the field in an unfamiliar town. Pulling up to a red light at a backed-up intersection, Holly berates herself: I'll be late and miss the start of the game. I'm the worst mother. Why can't I get my act together? The other mothers get there on time. Her jaw clenches, and she reminds herself to loosen it before it starts to ache.

Holly pulls into the parking lot, spotting the team's blue-and-gold uniforms. Her stomach gurgles as she takes a quick sip of cold coffee. Holly's running late because she offered to show a house for a colleague. She could have said no, but what about being a team player? Holly never knows where to draw the line.

For a moment Holly starts to relax, relieved she found her way and optimistic her clients will make an offer on a listing. She flashes back to the unwashed breakfast dishes soaking in the sink, the unfolded clothes wrinkling in the basket, the unanswered messages on her desk. The confidence, which she felt only a moment ago, has evaporated like a mirage in the desert.

Holly wishes she could hold onto the good feelings. But they never last. Now she has to face the other moms. They're nice, really. Yet, Holly has this ache inside her, like she doesn't fit in. She can't join the easy chatter.

Holly pulls her folding chair from the car and joins the other parents, as her nagging, critical voice plays in her head. All she wanted to do was come to this game, see her daughter play, and maybe get to know some other parents.

"Hi, Holly, how's it going?" asks Olivia, the mother of one of Sophie's long-time teammates. Olivia's expression is friendly, and she's surrounded by a group of loyal soccer moms. Holly puts on her well-worn game face. They would never understand.

"I'm great! Thanks for asking!"

Will Holly ever stop hearing this voice in her head? Will it ever end?

What do you notice about Holly? She's good at her job. She has a family. On the surface, Holly seems to be a successful woman living a good life. Yet, inside, Holly feels unsure of herself, never satisfied with who she is or what she's done, constantly faulting herself for her flaws. She longs to connect with other women but can't seem to figure out how to do that. Did any of Holly's struggles ring true for you? Take a moment to reflect on Holly's story and your reactions to it. This is a good time to take out your journal. You can write full sentences or jot down words or phrases that come to mind. Remember: there's no right way to do this!

At first glance, you may feel you have nothing in common with Holly. However, many daughters of narcissistic mothers find common feelings, thoughts, memories, behaviors, and impulses show up for them. You feel isolated and alone, overwhelmed with worry. You want to feel better, but don't know where to start. Here are common challenges you may face.

Difficulties setting healthy boundaries. Holly does a favor for her colleague when she really wants to leave for her daughter's soccer game. Similarly, perhaps you struggle to set limits or stand up for yourself. You know you should, but it's so difficult. On top of it, you feel powerless, angry, and guilty in the face of these decisions.

Believing the critical voice in your head. Holly hears a litany of perceived mistakes and weaknesses, from the past and the present, inside her mind. They feel like cold, hard facts. It may be hard for you to know whether the voice is your own or your mother's. Perhaps by now they are one and the same.

Shame and secret keeping. Holly pushes down her pain and keeps it to herself. You may have a "face" you show to the world while inside you feel alone and diminished. You isolate yourself and feel ashamed, as if you are on the outside looking in. Does anyone really know your true self?

Physical symptoms of stress. When Holly feels overwhelmed, stressed, or unsure, her body reacts in predictable ways: the muscles in her neck tighten up, her stomach burns, and her heart pounds. You likely also feel the impact of your emotions in your body. These symptoms not only make it harder to get through the day but also intensify your critical inner voice. You wonder why you can't manage stress better.

Repetitive negative thinking. Holly struggles to be in the present moment. Like Holly, your mind drifts to past negative events or to worries about the future. You worry that nothing you do is good enough. It's like being caught in a trap that you can't get out of. You feel unhappy and irritable. Even worse, it makes you more critical of the people you care about most. You try to push away your thoughts and memories and bad feelings, but it doesn't work. It's like living next to a construction site, where the jackhammers are going twenty-four hours a day, seven days a week.

Feeling alone and isolated with problems. Holly dreads Thanksgiving, Christmas, and especially Mother's Day, when her friends are excited to see their families. You know the feeling: buying a Mother's Day card should be a simple errand. Instead, you feel frozen and sick. You feel alone and that something is wrong with you as a daughter. Maybe something is wrong with you, period.

Second-guessing. To Holly, it seems like other women are so sure of themselves: they have strong opinions and don't hesitate to say what they think. Like Holly, you have strong opinions, alright, but then you hear that critical voice in your head: *Don't get too big for your britches! What do you know?*

Living for others. Holly finds herself doing "everything" for her kids, such as making their beds and packing their backpacks, tasks she knows they should do for themselves to become independent and responsible. If you are a mother, you also may struggle like Holly. You never want your kids to feel the way you did growing up: unimportant, uncared for, even invisible or scared. Are you like your mother? That's the hardest question.

Reading about Holly's experiences and considering the ways they relate with your own may cause uncomfortable thoughts, emotions, or memories to arise. That's where the next practice, Grounding with Five Senses, comes in. It's a mindfulness practice, which means you're focusing on the present moment instead of past problems or future worries. We use our senses, in the here and now, to shift gears and calm our nervous systems. The idea isn't to escape our thoughts and feelings. Instead, the idea is to notice them without trying to change, escape, or push them away. If you prefer to listen to this practice, you can find it on the website for this book, http://www.newharbinger.com/50096.

Practice: Grounding with Five Senses

To begin, take a few slow, deep breaths. Notice your belly rise as you breathe in and fall back as you breathe out. If you like, place a hand on your belly. Breathe in through your nose and out through your lips, as if you are gently blowing out a candle.

Press the bottoms of your feet firmly into the floor beneath you. Notice the connection between your feet and the floor, in your toes, in the balls of your feet, in the arches of your feet, and in your heels.

Gently shift your attention to your *eyes*. What do you see with your eyes? Look around and name three things, even the smallest thing you notice with your eyes. Perhaps an object in the room, a slant of light, or a tree outside the window.

Next, what do you hear with your *ears*? Focus on three sounds, even the slightest sounds you notice with your ears. Perhaps a bird outside, the creak of the floor, your own breathing.

Consider what you smell with your *nose*. Focus on three things you notice with your nose. Perhaps last night's dinner, the carpet, the inside of your nose.

Pay attention to what you feel with your *body or skin*. Focus on three things you notice with your body or skin. Perhaps the chair beneath you, the watch on your wrist, the hair on the back of your neck.

What do you taste with your *mouth?* Focus on three things you notice with your mouth. Perhaps your toothpaste, your coffee, your own mouth.

Now, gently return to your breathing. Take a few more slow, deep breaths. Press your feet into the floor. Return to your normal state of attention.

How did it feel to do this exercise? What did you notice? What was challenging about this exercise? What was easiest? If you like, write these answers in your journal.

During the next week, try to practice Grounding with Five Senses every day, at least once a day when you are feeling calm. Daily practice develops the skill of *noticing*. When you notice what you see, hear, smell, touch, and taste and get comfortable with that, you can shift to noticing your emotions, which is more challenging. Second, it's important to practice when you feel calm so it's easier to do this when you're not. It's why we have fire drills—we don't wait until there's a fire to figure out how to safely exit the building. It's helpful to schedule a time to practice and put it in your calendar to remind you. Think about what time works best for you. Now that you've practiced noticing with your five senses, in the next section you'll practice doing an inventory of your experiences.

Take Inventory of Your Experience

As you read the stories in this book, you may be surprised that you have little in common with the women discussed in terms of your life experiences and background. Nonetheless, the ways you feel *inside* are probably remarkably similar. Here is a checklist of problems and feelings you may experience. Please read through it and record those that resonate with you. This is a good time to keep your journal handy so you can write down any thoughts, feelings, or memories that emerge. You don't need to write in full sentences. Just jot down thoughts, phrases, or images. If you prefer, draw your feelings. You may find that completing the inventory triggers sensitive emotions or memories. That's normal. Take your time.

- ☐ Think over and over about worries

- ☐ Isolate myself, even if I want to spend time with others

- ☐ Feel I don't deserve good things to happen to me, even if I work hard for them

- ☐ Withdraw from my mother, then feel guilty

- ☐ Feel I can never do enough

- ☐ Take on too many responsibilities

- ☐ Try to get my mother to appreciate or understand me, even though it never works

- ☐ Question myself and doubt my judgments or decisions

- ☐ Try to do everything perfectly

- ☐ Have trouble getting close to people

- ☐ Feel "different" from other women

- ☐ Have difficulty trusting people

- ☐ Second-guess myself, which makes me more anxious

- ☐ Don't know what I'm feeling and can't put my feelings into words

- ☐ Excuse other people's bad behavior and get into relationships that aren't good for me

☐ Stuff my feelings, then blow up

☐ Feel that my emotions don't matter or aren't as important as other people's

☐ Feel ashamed and embarrassed about my relationship with my mother

☐ Feel responsible for my mother's happiness

☐ Feel angry that my mother ignores me when I do set limits

☐ Feel scared or threatened by my mother's behavior

☐ Worry about how my mother's behavior will affect other people, such as my children or spouse

☐ Think I will feel relieved when my mother dies, then feel like a horrible person for feeling this way

On top of all of this, I feel:

☐ It's my fault for feeling this way.

☐ There's something wrong with me.

☐ I can't tell anyone how I feel.

What did you notice as you completed the checklist? Did anything surprise you, even if you didn't feel much at all? It's common for daughters of narcissistic mothers to have difficulty identifying their feelings and putting them into words because it's likely your emotions went unnoticed or were criticized or even demeaned. We'll go into this in depth in chapter 7. For now, here are some ways to figure out what you're feeling.

1. Please go to the website for this book, http://www.newharbinger .com/50096, for a list of emotion words. See if you can find words that describe the emotion or emotions you're having right now, and write them down in your journal. If you don't feel

anything, see if you can put words to that, such as "numb" or "distanced."

2. Keep a list of emotion words or a feelings wheel at the ready (which you can find online). A feelings wheel depicts "shades" or levels of feelings. Just like a color strip from a paint store has multiple shades of blue, emotions have multiple shades and words to define them.

3. Pick one feeling per week to practice becoming aware of. Let's say you choose sad. Try to notice the following information and log it as follows in your journal:

What are you feeling?

What is the situation?

What happened before?

What happened after?

Write down the thoughts you had.

Write down what you felt in your body.

Identify a more precise word for your feeling (you can refer to a feelings wheel to help you). For example, are you lonely, bored, inadequate, miserable?

Does finding a more precise word for your feeling make a difference in understanding your emotional state, the situation, or your actions? How?

You're becoming an explorer in your unique emotional territory. Research shows that the better we get at labeling the "shades" of our emotions, the better we get at managing our reactions to our emotions. This, in turn, helps us get our needs met *and* be more empathetic to other people (Brackett 2019). As with any skill, identifying your emotions gets easier with practice. It also gets less overwhelming because your emotional "dictionary" will expand.

Let's return to Holly's story. Here's how an interaction with her mother unfolds *before* she has done the inner work in this book.

The following week, Holly pulls into the parking lot at the soccer field when her phone rings. The caller ID indicates it's her mother, Natalie. Holly wonders if today could be different, with her mother acting supportive, caring, and interested. Yet, she knows she'll be frustrated and hurt. I'm not up for this. I can't handle this. *Holly hesitates, then reaches for the phone.*

"Hi, Mom. What's up? I'm on my way to Sophie's game. It's about to start." Here we go again. *Holly's heart pounds. Sweat trickles down her neck.*

Natalie scoffs. "You're always in a hurry. I was never like that when you were growing up. You know, if you were more organized, this probably wouldn't happen. You always were so messy." Her mother's voice is sharp as she makes her pronouncement on Holly's life, comparing it to her own. Natalie is a beloved elementary school principal. Holly can't reach for a head of lettuce at the grocery store or fill her minivan with gas without someone telling her how wonderful her mother is, how understanding, how involved, how kind.

Holly feels a familiar wave wash over her. Of what? Sadness, guilt, shame—feeling bad about herself. Just once, she wishes her mother could recognize how hard she works and that she is doing a good job of handling work, the kids, the whole shebang.

"Do you need something, Mom? We'll see you on Sunday for dinner." Holly's words are firm, but she feels hollow, as if her insides have been scooped out like a pumpkin on Halloween. Her foot taps the car floor.

"No, I'm fine. I just didn't know what you want me to cook. I need to shop. But it's not important. Bye."

Now let's look at the same encounter, after Holly has come to value and take care of herself.

When Holly pulls up to a red light at a backed-up intersection, she begins the familiar reprimand: I'll probably be late and miss the start of the game. I'm the worst mother. Why can't I get my act together?

Holly takes a breath at the red light. She notices those thoughts but doesn't take them seriously. They're like the cars speeding by on the other side of the road, the ones not stuck at the red light. She can't stop or control them. She can just notice them as they drive by.

Holly pulls into the parking lot, where she can see her daughter's game about to begin. Then her phone rings. It's her mother, Natalie. She recognizes her feeling of self-blame show up, what she used to think was just garden-variety stress. She places her hands in her lap and takes a few deep breaths: Breathe in for the count of three. Breathe out for the count of six. If there's one thing I've learned when it comes to dealing with Mom, it's to wait. *Pause. Holly's heart rate slows down. The tension in her neck loosens.*

Once her heart rate has slowed down, she can handle her thoughts better. She reminds herself that conversations with her mother are frustrating. Her mother will not change, but Holly has changed how she deals with her. A wave of sadness passes over Holly. How she wishes things were different. Now she knows these painful feelings about her mother may always be part of her life. But they don't have to stop her from living the life she wants. Right now, this time is for me and Sophie, *she decides.*

Holly presses Decline Call, drops her cell phone in her purse, and unhooks her seatbelt. Grabbing her folding chair from the back seat, she heads to the game. As she settles in next to the other parents, Holly imagines enclosing her time at the soccer game in an imaginary bubble that belongs to her. She'll call Mom later.

Quickly, Holly is lost in the game as she cheers for her daughter's team and chats excitedly about their plays with the other parents. She pets the warm fur of a dog that settles between her and the next chair and dips her head back into the sun.

That evening, after dinner and homework are done, Holly sinks down in the sofa while her husband, Joe, finishes the dishes. She listens to some relaxing music. Preparing to return her mother's call, Holly thinks about how to handle the call with her mother. She used to just react to her mother's behavior and had no idea what was good for her. Now she checks in with her inner voice. She used to just hear Natalie's voice. Holly pauses; she can hear her own voice and knows the right thing to do.

Holly reminds herself that her mother's narcissistic behaviors are painful, but she doesn't have to suffer from them like she once did. No matter how hard she tries to be the perfect daughter, Natalie won't feel happy or tell Holly that she approves of her or is proud of her. Holly remembers to listen to her mother but not to try to fix things. Before she places the call, Holly recalls the times she's already handled phone calls with her mother with greater ease. She's learned that her mother can say unkind things and Holly can feel okay.

"Hi Mom. I'm returning your call. What's up?"

"I called you this afternoon!"

"I know. I was at Sophie's soccer game. I was so proud of her. She played hard. She's getting better all the time."

"Hmmph. Do I get to come to a game sometime? Janie Richards takes her mother to Kelsey's games every Saturday." Holly feels a spike of anxiety remembering the last time Natalie came to one of Sophie's soccer games. Natalie complained that it was too hot and too buggy. The chair Holly brought for Natalie was uncomfortable. Her mother felt "ignored" when Holly talked to her friends.

"Gee, Mom. Thanks for asking about that. I'll take a look at the schedule." Holly has no intention of ever taking her mother to another of Sophie's games. She's also learned that her mother cannot have a reasonable conversation about what happened the last time—about her own behavior and how it impacted Holly. They can't problem solve so things can go better next time because Natalie continues to say things like, "That never happened! I don't know what you're talking about!"

In the past, those kinds of conversations with her mother made Holly doubt herself and her own view of reality. Now that she understands narcissistic behavior, Holly trusts herself. Now, Holly's brain and gut instinct tell Holly to set a limit by gently deflecting her mother. Other times she needs to be much firmer, and when she needs to, she can.

"Fine," spits out Holly's mother. "Did you hear that Janie got a big promotion at work? I can't remember what she does, but she makes a lot of money. Have you sold any houses lately?"

"You know, Mom, I've told you that I don't want to discuss my finances with you. Please don't ask me about that." Holly has worked hard to speak up and set this limit with her mother. She also understands that it is no surprise that Natalie has such difficulty connecting to her daughter. Natalie's own mother died when she was ten years old. Her father quickly remarried a woman with two children of her own, and the families did not blend well. Natalie felt alone and ignored.

"I can't ever reach you," her mother continues. "You're so busy! Doing what, I don't know. How can I know what to make for dinner on Sunday? Is Sophie still so picky?" Holly smiles to herself. Her mother's narcissistic behavior is so predictable: Holly spoke her mind and set a limit. Natalie changed the subject. No acknowledgment. No apology.

"Well, you know we love your lasagna," says Holly. "We'll come at six like we always do, and I'll bring the salad. See you then. Bye, Mom."

Holly hangs up the phone and tells Joe she's going for a walk. She knows that dealing with her mother will never be easy. She will always need to be self-aware and prepare and practice for their interactions. Still, at this stage in her life, Holly feels free and separate from her mother.

Holly learned how narcissism impacted her mother's behavior. For example, she learned that people with narcissistic traits can show a kind of superficial empathy for other peoples' feelings. Sometimes they can't show any empathy at all. Those unpredictable behaviors made Holly feel confused and anxious when she was growing up, although she didn't understand why at the time. Most important, Holly learned that although her mother's behavior was unlikely to change, Holly could change, and that was all that mattered.

Understanding what narcissism is all about was key to Holly's capacity to move forward, and we'll cover that in more detail in the next two chapters. For now, here are several ways in which Holly learned to feel calm and confident, even though her mother's behavior did not change.

Holly identifies her feelings and works toward accepting them, even the painful ones. Holly learned that she can't control what she thinks and feels. Her thoughts and feelings aren't good or bad; they just are. She doesn't have to feel ashamed of them or that she has to stop having them in order to have a good life.

Holly makes choices based on who and what's important to her. Instead of getting caught up in her thoughts and feelings about her mother, she focuses on what she cares about and what she can actually do to make a difference. Now, when Holly goes to soccer games, her "I don't belong here" thoughts still show up sometimes. However, Holly notices them and decides to sit next to the other parents and fully participate anyway.

Holly trusts her judgment. It helps that she knows she doesn't have to be perfect. She can do her best. If a choice does not work out, she can try again.

Holly no longer jumps when her mother says jump. She's learned that saying no isn't wrong; it's essential for her well-being and survival. She's learned new ways to communicate with Natalie that feel both firm and respectful. This style of assertiveness has helped Holly in many parts of her life, not just with her mother.

Holly focuses on her strengths. When she feels shaky, she thinks about times in the past she handled difficult situations. Holly remembered when the children were in preschool and Joe was away on a week-long business trip. She and the kids came down with a stomach bug. Holly remembers feeling so awful and overwhelmed. But she handled it, even asking a neighbor for help, who dropped off ginger ale and crackers. Recalling this challenge reminds Holly that she is resourceful. She can be strong, even when she feels at her worst. This strategy increases her self-worth and problem-solving skills.

Holly takes care of herself. Rather than just caring for others and her job, Holly gets enough sleep, eats properly, moves her body, and spends time with friends.

Holly notices how she has internalized her mother's critical voice but is no longer hopelessly entangled with it. When it starts to play, Holly recognizes it for what it is. Sometimes Holly thinks of her mother's voice like clouds in the sky drifting by. Sometimes she "talks" to it: *I expected you to show up today. That's fine, but I don't have to listen to you. I'm done with that.*

Holly trusts her inner voice. When it comes to dealing with her mother and other parts of her life, she draws on her gut instincts and sense of what's right for her.

With these tools, Holly's inner voice has grown stronger and clearer than her mother's. You can learn these tools also. It can be painful to reflect on your past experiences with your mother. You might feel sad, anxious, guilty, angry, or relieved, to name just a few possible emotions. But simply by reading the first chapter and completing the inventory of your experiences, you've begun a process of self-reflection and, yes, even change.

You've taken the first steps to understanding yourself, your mother, and the road to change. Hopefully, you feel less alone in your experiences as the daughter of a narcissistic mother. The next chapter will help you make sense of who your mother is. We'll unpack the complex topic of narcissism and the confusing ways it can show up in mothers.

Chapter 2

Understanding Your Mother

It's been difficult to understand your mother. Her personality was simply what you knew growing up, and you had nothing to compare it to. As an adult, you had a problem that people don't talk about. To add to the mystery, when you are raised by a narcissistic mother, you learn to tune your attention to others instead of yourself. You learn to doubt your own perceptions and ideas. How, then, can you develop a true understanding of your mother's personality and behavior, which is a key step toward creating a more calm and confident sense of yourself?

In this chapter, you'll get an overview of narcissism. As you read about what makes your mother tick, perhaps it will help you, little by little, to realize that your mother's behaviors and attitudes belonged to her. They were not your fault. You did not cause them. Nor can you change them. However, you can understand them, with the goal of understanding their impact on you so you can build a more rich and meaningful life.

What a Healthy Sense of Identity Is Like

Before we talk about what narcissism is, it's helpful to understand what it is not. A non-narcissistic adult has a secure sense of who they are inside, what the mental health profession calls a *sense of identity* (American Psychiatric Association 2013). Adults with reasonably secure identities:

- know what's important to them and have direction in life

- understand their feelings and empathize with the feelings of others

- can have close relationships with others

- can handle conflict in relationships.

When you have a healthy sense of self or identity, you know what your strengths are, feel good about them, and can put them to work in your life. You also know what your weaknesses are and accept them. You don't feel like a failure because you're not good at everything. You don't fall apart or fly into a rage when a weakness comes to light (say, for example, you struggle with spelling and your boss points out several typos in your PowerPoint presentation). You can handle it because your inner sense of self is both strong and flexible enough to absorb that criticism. You might feel bad or uncomfortable when your boss highlights your mistake. Nobody likes to be criticized! However, you take your sense of self, brush yourself off, and develop a plan: perhaps you'll ask a colleague to proofread your slides in the future. And you move on. In addition, people with a secure inner identity can name and respond to their feelings in appropriate ways. This is not easy to do, even for the most mature of us. These combined abilities are often referred to as "emotion regulation."

Someone with a secure sense of identity is like an earthquake-proof building. Buildings in earthquake-prone areas are constructed with flexible materials that spread out the shocks received during quakes. Buildings constructed to survive earthquakes can *bend without breaking.* Just like an earthquake-proof building, this person is flexible: She can bend, especially under stress, without coming apart at the seams. She's open to other people's ideas, perspectives, and feelings.

What Is Narcissism?

In contrast, there is *narcissism.* It's a broad topic, and like many areas of psychology, mental health professionals have several perspectives on it. In this book, we'll look at information that helps you understand your mother. At their core, narcissistic mothers, like all narcissists, are driven by "pathological insecurity" (Durvasula 2021). We're all insecure sometimes, especially if we were raised by a narcissist. However, a narcissist is unaware of how her fragile self-esteem drives her behavior. She's unaware that her need to be number one, or constantly cared for by others, fuels how she treats other people. She feels entitled to special treatment. When she doesn't receive this, she reacts in a variety of ways, from becoming enraged and attacking to becoming depressed and needy. All these reactions spring from the emptiness inside her.

Narcissism is a personality style composed of a constellation of traits and behaviors. If you think of a whole personality like a unique jigsaw puzzle, then the individual puzzle pieces are the personality traits. They fit together, creating a picture of the person. An outgoing, friendly, and easy-going friend has pops of bright colors. An introverted, quiet, more sensitive friend picture has more muted shades. When it comes to the narcissism puzzle, let's pay attention to a few key pieces. You may recognize some of the following behaviors or personality traits common to people with narcissism (adapted from Fox 2018):

- Takes advantage of others to achieve her own goals

- Reacts to criticism with rage

- Has excessive feelings of self-importance

- Exaggerates achievements and talents

- Is preoccupied with power and success fantasies

- Has unreasonable expectations of favorable treatment

- Needs constant attention and admiration

- Exhibits obsessive self-interest

- Pursues mainly selfish goals

Narcissism occurs on a *spectrum*. That means your mother may have had a few narcissistic traits and behaviors that impacted her functioning somewhat. She may have had a lot of them that showed up all the time, in almost all situations in her life.

The most extreme and inflexible form of narcissism is called "narcissistic personality disorder" or NPD. NPD occurs in approximately 1 to 2 percent of the population. Whether your mother's narcissistic traits and behaviors came and went or whether she had full-blown NPD, the impact of unhealthy narcissism can take a heavy toll.

When Janelle came to therapy, she described how weary she was of not trusting people, even her own children. This was becoming increasingly difficult as her children were teenagers and spending more time with their friends, away from Janelle and her husband. Her once-chatty children spent their time at home behind closed doors, their ever-present earbuds blocking out Janelle's attempts at conversation. Janelle felt she didn't know what was going on with her children, as she did when they were younger, so she was always second-guessing them. This made her extremely anxious and led to meddling. Janelle knew her behavior (such as wanting to stay at the movies with her kids) could hurt her relationship with her teens, but she couldn't stop.

Janelle connected the dots to her own upbringing by a mother who was warm and available when Janelle was doing well in school and sports and was angry and critical when Janelle got a bad grade or didn't make captain of a team. Janelle learned she could never trust which mother she was going to get, and that anxiety was stuck inside her. She wanted to be there for her children at all times so they always knew she loved them. But sometimes that instinct set her off course.

We'll look at how all these puzzle pieces play out in ways that may resonate with you. I will share one common dynamic at a time by telling a story of a mother-daughter pair, asking you to reflect on how it relates to your experience, and then offering an exercise you can do as part of your own healing journey. This way, as you gain clarity on your mother's behavior, you will also gain access to how you truly feel. At heart, I do this so the book always stays focused on you and how you are affected by a narcissistic mother. My hope is that, as a result, you can also stay focused on *you*.

Adult or Adolescent?

Kara's mother, Lydia, loved to dress like Kara. Wearing matching mother-daughter outfits was fine when Kara was in kindergarten. However, Lydia continued this tradition as Kara entered high school. Kara was mortified when her mother headed out for a night of drinking, wearing a pair of skinny jeans plucked from Kara's closet.

"I know these are your favorite jeans, but don't you think they look better on me?" Lydia inquired.

Kara's parents were long divorced, and Kara was mortified when Lydia began dating a nineteen-year-old guy who had just graduated from high school. Kara asked her mother to stop dating him, at least until Kara left for college.

"It's my life," retorted Lydia, sliding her iPhone into her back pocket. "Sorry if you don't like it." Kara felt furious and invisible at the same time.

Lydia's mother died when she was ten years old. After her mother's death, her father worked long hours. At school, Lydia drifted from group to group, never finding a place to fit in. As Kara's mother, she's still trying to grow up and find a sense of identity that never had a chance to get started. Lydia's story illustrates a common struggle among narcissists, one that impacts their daughters in myriad ways. Lydia doesn't know whether she's an adult or an adolescent. Without a chance to be a teenager at the appropriate time, she remains stuck. Lydia certainly has no idea how her lack of an adult identity impacted her daughter.

Kara's mother lacked what the mental health profession calls a fully developed "sense of self." Lydia looked like an adult on the outside but was a much younger person on the inside. Lydia often behaved like she was in middle school. Sometimes Kara felt as if she were dealing with a three-year-old having a tantrum when she didn't get her way. Lydia had no self-awareness about her own behavior, let alone how it impacted her daughter. She had no capacity to empathize with her daughter's feelings. This is simply one example of how Kara felt unloved and unseen throughout her life.

As you read this story, what thoughts, emotions, physical sensations in your body, or memories came up for you? Please write them down in your journal. Remember you don't have to use full sentences. You can draw if you prefer.

- Do you have any new insights about your mother?

- Do you have any new insights about yourself?

- What is your most important takeaway from this section?

If you're struggling to connect with your experience as you read, I'd like to share a way of becoming aware of the moment. In the introduction to this book, I wrote that you don't have to formally meditate in order to become more mindful: that is, to set aside a period of time to sit and focus on your breath. But it's worth a try. Here's why. Our breath is always with us and always changing. It's a "convenient" way to become more aware of our daily thoughts, feelings, and experiences. Jon Kabat-Zinn (1990), founder of Mindfulness-Based Stress Reduction, explains that by "focusing on the breath when we meditate, we are learning right from the start to get comfortable with change. We see that we have to be flexible" (49).

The good news is that you can learn to focus on your breath in your own way. You can start with one minute per day if you like, or five, or more. Try it out for yourself by reading the following directions to yourself or listening to the recording at http://www.newharbinger.com/50096.

Practice: Mindful Moment

Sit up straight with your legs crossed comfortably or your feet on the floor. If you prefer, you can lie down. Allow your eyes to close if it's comfortable to you.

Pay attention to your belly, noticing your belly rise with the inhale and fall back with exhale. Gently follow the path of the breath, in and out, in and out, along with the rise and fall of your belly.

When your mind wanders off, which it will, gently bring your attention back to your breathing. It doesn't matter how many times that happens. The job, in fact, is "starting over," having a chance to begin again no matter how far afield your thoughts and feelings wander, or how often.

As Kabat-Zinn (1990) explains: "It is remarkable how liberating it feels to be able to see that your thoughts are just thoughts and that they are not 'you' or 'reality'" (69). After you practice this breathing meditation, write about your experiences in your journal.

Lack of Self-Direction

Jackie's mother, Abby, constantly quit her jobs in financial services. At first, the job was perfect. Her boss loved her! They really "got" each other! Within a few months, Abby found her perfect job disappointing. The deadlines were insane. People were rude and uncooperative. Her boss did not appreciate how hard she worked and her unique ideas. How could anyone survive a job like that? Abby grew angrier and angrier, and then she quit. Abby didn't realize that being successful in her job took persistent effort; sometimes she would have to struggle as she learned new skills. Being successful would not magically happen because she was special.

Growing up, initially when Abby got a new job, Jackie loved watching her mother get dressed up for work. They packed their lunches together in the morning. Eventually, Jackie stayed quiet when Abby exclaimed about her new jobs, trying her best to stay invisible as Jackie imagined her success. It pained Jackie as she prepared for what was sure to come: Abby's angry rants, the morning's moping. It felt as if Abby's emotions were Jackie's too, settling inside her like fog in the rain.

The opposite scenario can also reflect a mother's struggles with self-direction. Gail, Ashley's mother, never made it to a job at all. Ashley's father, Roger, was the CEO of a Fortune 500 company. Gail frequently traveled with Roger on his business trips around the world. When home, she played tennis and volunteered. Ashley and her older sister, Alicia, stayed with the nanny, cook, and housekeeper. Then came the recession and the banking crisis. The family downsized; the nanny, cook, and housekeeper were let go, but Gail announced she would never go back to work. "I can't be on a schedule!"

Both Abby and Gail struggled with self-direction. Neither mother had the capacity to cope with the ups and downs of the working world. Both they and their daughters paid the price. It is unlikely that Abby and Gail had a clear sense of who they were, just like Lydia struggled with her identity. As such, they struggled to find rewarding work and have the emotional strength needed to stay the course.

When you have not seen self-direction modeled in your mother, you may be someone who pushes yourself to your breaking points. You feel as if you can never do enough. On the outside, it might seem as if you have it all together. But inside, it's as if there's an inner pressure cooker inside you, always on the verge of exploding.

Or perhaps, you just can't seem to find your way. You drift from one thing to another, unable to commit to a path. You might have interests and talents, but nothing really sticks or gels as if you are sort of empty inside.

As you read through this section, what thoughts, emotions, physical sensations in your body, or memories came up for you? Please write them down in your journal. Remember you don't have to use full sentences. You can draw if you prefer.

- Do you have any new insights about your mother?

- Do you have any new insights about yourself?

- What is your most important takeaway from this section?

Knowing what you value most can help you gain a sense of direction for how you want to live. Acceptance and commitment therapy (ACT) defines values as your life's guiding principles. "They are the way you want to be in life and the way you want to act toward others, the world, and yourself," says Marisa Mazza (2020, 43), author of *The ACT Workbook for OCD*. Values live inside your heart; they're like your personal North Star or inner compass. Our values help us create a meaningful life. While our values live in our hearts, they must be paired with concrete actions to create that life. Values can't thrive in a vacuum. They exist in the real world.

Values are different from goals, although values shape and inform our goals. A goal has an end point; it can be completed. A value is never-ending. Let's look at an example so you can see how defining your values can help you. In this context, values are *not* about morals, or right and wrong. The simplest way to think about values is: What do you value in life?

Battling Boundaries

Sabrina struggled to set limits with her mother, Marian. Sabrina was forty, unmarried, and worked long hours as an emergency department physician. Sabrina lived twenty minutes away from Marian, while her two her brothers, both who were married with families, lived several hours away. If she wasn't working, Sabrina went to her mother's condo every Sunday afternoon, swinging by the grocery store or pharmacy on the way. Sabrina cooked dinner, tidied up, and maybe ran a load of laundry. Marian had arthritis and told Sabrina she simply couldn't do these tasks. Yet, somehow during the week, she played bridge with her friends, walked her dog, and gardened. On the few occasions Sabrina didn't go on her day off, Marian sent her curt, insulting emails that hurt Sabrina deeply, remarking, "You always have time for your patients." Sabrina's friends encouraged her to take time for herself. But when Sabrina read those emails from her mother, she felt cut to the core, and flooded with guilt, shame, and anxiety. Sometimes she felt angry, and then she felt guilty for feeling angry at her mother. Then Sabrina got a wake-up call at her annual physical. Her blood pressure was off the charts, and she was prediabetic. Sabrina decided she had to do something different.

For Sabrina, defining her values, and specific behaviors to enact them, was not easy.

Sabrina's values. Taking care of my health and body, being considerate of myself, being considerate of others, being adventurous, connecting with new people, asking for help.

Sabrina's goals. Going to the gym three times a week, joining a hiking club and attending at least once a month, requesting my brothers set up and monitor online grocery delivery for Mom, visiting Mom every three weeks with phone calls in between.

Defining her values brought up painful feelings for Sabrina, such as guilt, shame, and self-doubt. She needed to learn to handle those emotions, and we'll see how she did that.

Practice: Define Your Values

Values tend to fall within domains (Walser and Westrup 2007). Please write what your values are in each of the following eight domains. It can be surprisingly difficult to come up with your values, so I created an exercise called the "Values Pie" that you can download at http://www.newharbin ger.com/50096. Defining your values is one of the first steps in creating a meaningful life that reflects who you are and how you want to live. Below is the list of values, which is inspired by the work of Walser and Westrup (2007) and is also seen in the "Values Pie." This is a good time to take out your journal and write down your values, based on the list below.

1. Intimate relationship and marriage values

2. Family relationships and parenting values

3. Friendship values

4. Contributing to community values

5. Education, work, and career values

6. Physical well-being values

7. Recreation and fun values

8. Spirituality values

As you read through the section on self-direction, what thoughts, emotions, physical sensations in your body, or memories came up for you? Please write them down in your journal. Remember you don't have to use full sentences. You can draw if you prefer.

- Do you have any new insights about your mother?

- Do you have any new insights about yourself?

- What is your most important takeaway from this section?

Constant Criticism

Aubrey, daughter of a narcissistic mother, struggled with her weight since childhood. Sitting across from her therapist, Aubrey clenches her fists, comforted by the pinch of her nails in her palms. "I dreaded shopping for my clothes with my mother. She insisted on coming into the dressing room with me, even when I was a teenager! I couldn't stand it. I asked her once to wait outside, and she threw a fit like there was something wrong with me for wanting privacy. I wanted to wear what the other girls were wearing, and that was practically impossible."

"I remember trying on these denim shorts with fringe and rhinestones that were really popular," Aubrey continued. "My mother took one look at them and said, 'Your butt is hanging out.' It was so crude. But you know, looking back, I think a little part of her enjoyed it. Sometimes I would see a little smile on her face. I don't think she felt that great about herself either. Why couldn't she have said, 'Those are probably not the best choice'? Aubrey crossed her arm across her stomach and continued.

"We went to the town pool every summer. I loved to swim! One day, I overheard a woman tell my mother what a 'cute little belly' I had. The next thing I know, my mother ran over to me. She yanked me by the hand and made me put on a T-shirt. For the rest of the summer, she made me wear it at the pool. It was so uncomfortable and embarrassing. Swimming was no fun after that."

Like many narcissistic mothers, Aubrey's mother's self-esteem—her sense of self—was as easily shattered as a crystal cup. She too struggled with weight as a child and carried her mother's harsh comments inside her. Aubrey's mother learned to wall off her painful feelings. This left her little ability to empathize with her daughter's, in spite of the struggle they shared.

It's likely Aubrey's mother was flooded with feelings of shame and anger in that dressing room, leading her to shame Aubrey about her body.

The mother who has difficulties with empathy (really, all narcissistic mothers) struggles to recognize and truly understand her daughter's feelings and needs. In contrast, she's acutely sensitive to how other people make her feel. Her internal radar constantly searches for compliments or criticism. As you read through this section, what thoughts, emotions, physical sensations in your body, or memories came up for you? Please write them down in your journal. Remember you don't have to use full sentences. You can draw if you prefer.

- Do you have any new insights about your mother?

- Do you have any new insights about yourself?

- What is your most important takeaway from this section?

You likely learned to speak to yourself as critically as your mother spoke to you. Fortunately, talking to ourselves with kindness can be learned. Not only can it be learned, but thousands of research studies have demonstrated that doing so improves our emotional and even physical well-being. It is an essential skill for daughters in managing that critical inner voice. Mindful self-compassion (MSC), which was developed by Kristin Neff, PhD, and Christopher Germer, PhD, is based on three principles (Neff and Germer 2018):

Self-kindness vs. self-judgment. Self-kindness means talking to yourself, when you are struggling, the same way you would talk to someone you care about. Most of us, and certainly daughters of narcissistic mothers, know exactly how to berate and beat ourselves up in our minds. When we fall short or make a mistake, we say things to ourselves we would never say to a friend or loved one, probably things we would never even say to a stranger. It may be your own voice or your mother's voice. Or perhaps the voices are so mixed up that it's hard to distinguish them. MSC proposes a radical flip of the switch: addressing yourself with kindness, compassion, support, and encouragement.

Common humanity. This means acknowledging that it is normal to feel emotional pain, to make mistakes, to have problems. It is a core part of being human. We're not alone in our suffering, and we're not alone in our imperfections or the ways we mess things up.

Mindfulness. As we know, mindfulness means experiencing our thoughts, emotions, and sensations in the here and now without judging or criticizing them. This is the first step in viewing those thoughts, emotions, and sensations with kindness and compassion.

Practice: Cultivating a Kind Inner Voice

In your journal, please write the answers to the following questions.

- Think about a time a friend came to you with a problem, disappointment, or failure. Try to remember the time as fully as possible—what you saw, how you felt, the atmosphere.

- What did you say to your friend? How would you describe your tone of voice? If you were in person, did you touch your friend, and if so, how would you describe the quality of that touch?

- Think about a time when you had a problem, disappointment, or failure. What did you say to yourself? How would you describe your internal tone of voice? How did you treat yourself physically?

- Were there differences between the way you talked to your friend and the way you talked to yourself? If so, in what ways?

Over the next few weeks, notice these patterns when they come up. Also, were there times when you were able to talk to yourself with more kindness or compassion, even just a little bit? What were those times? What was happening? How does it make a difference for you when you talk to yourself with kindness and compassion? (Adapted from Neff and Germer, 2018.)

Struggling to Be Close

Maya recalls family dinners when her mother, Eve, a television producer, would talk on and on about her day. Her father, David, a reserved writer, would listen along with Maya and her brother, Peter. When David, Maya, or Peter introduced a subject, Eve would listen for a moment and boomerang the topic back to herself, "I studied that when I was in high school."

Even though Maya's family ate dinner together most nights, Maya never felt connected to her parents or brother. Eve's talking about herself barricaded closeness with her family. And, like most people with narcissistic traits, Eve had no awareness of the impact of her behavior. As adults, Maya and Peter struggled to make close connections with others and to feel valued in relationships.

What does it take to have a close mother-daughter relationship? If there were a recipe, what would the ingredients be? Over the past few decades, psychologists have identified essential ingredients for a healthy parent-child relationship, one that will foster closeness between mother and daughter.

The following list of "ingredients" is based on the ground breaking work of developmental psychologist Diana Baumrind (1967, used with permission of Taylor & Francis), who coined the term "authoritative parenting," or what I call "balanced parenting." Here are the ingredients of balanced parenting:

- Parents express warmth and are nurturing.

- Parents are in charge.

- Parents listen to children's points of view.

- Discipline is fair and not given in the heat of anger.

- Parents encourage their children's independence in ways that match their abilities.

- Parents handle their own emotions, especially challenging ones.

- Parents apologize and take responsibility when they make mistakes.

- Parents love and nurture the child they have, not the one they want.

- Parents create flexible structure and routines for their children.

Mothers with narcissistic traits struggle with knowing who they are as people. They cover up an inner world of insecurity with a veneer of self-importance and demanding behavior. Although they have the power to drown out their daughter's voice like a tidal wave, inside, their sense of self is as fragile as a moth's wings. They have difficulty knowing what they feel and handling their emotions, especially difficult ones, such as anger, sadness, and fear.

But some mothers with narcissistic traits may demonstrate some of these ingredients some of the time so their daughters learn to trust and feel safe opening up to them. Some mothers may have very few of these traits, very little of the time, making it far more likely that their daughters will isolate from them. Remember Aubrey, whose mother barged into the dressing room and made fun of her weight? Or Abby, whose struggle with work pained her daughter Jackie? These mother-daughter relationships were missing key ingredients to create a foundation of safety and closeness: fostering independence and the mother's ability to take care of herself.

Do Maya's experiences and feelings resonate for you? As you read through this section, what thoughts, emotions, physical sensations in your body, or memories came up for you? Please write them down in your journal. Remember you don't have to use full sentences. You can draw if you prefer.

- Do you have any new insights about your mother?

- Do you have any new insights about yourself?

- What is your most important takeaway from this section?

Many daughters of narcissistic mothers feel overwhelmed by anxious, self-critical thoughts about their difficult relationships with their mothers and themselves. They hear their mothers' critical voice, reciting their flaws and mistakes, blaming them for their problems in their relationships. To make matters worse, they feel as if they should be able to stop these thoughts. What's wrong with their minds?

Here's what's wrong with their minds: NOTHING. We simply can't stop or control our thoughts. Our minds produce thousands of thoughts per day. Trying to stop or control our thoughts is like trying to stop the waves in the ocean. It's like trying to stop a speeding train with a feather.

Simply knowing this fact provides relief for many daughters of narcissistic mothers. Once you know you can't stop or control your thoughts, you can develop a new relationship with them. Maybe you can even feel less guilty or inadequate for having the thoughts!

The metaphor of the ball in the pool from acceptance and commitment therapy, brings to life the idea that trying to stop our thoughts is ineffective and makes us feel worse. Here's an exercise to help you experience what happens when you stop fighting your negative thoughts and just permit them to be around.

Practice: Ball in the Pool

Imagine you're standing in the middle of a beautiful pool holding a beach ball. The beach ball is your unpleasant, painful emotions, thoughts, or memories. You don't want to have contact with these things, so you push the beach ball under the water. What happens? Of course, it pops right back up. You shove it under the water again. It pops back up. You do this over and over. Eventually, you get tired of pushing it under and having it pop back up. So, you decide to toss the beach ball aside in the pool.

What happens? The beach ball drifts here and there in the pool. Sometimes it floats near you. Sometimes it floats away. It's still in the pool. But now that you're not holding it, trying to push it down, you're free to swim, float, or do whatever you came into the pool to do. Please go to http://www.newharbin ger.com/50096 for a recording of the Ball in the Pool practice (Stoddard and Afari 2014).

In this chapter, you learned about the behaviors often engaged in by narcissists so you can identify them when they occur. You learned that you're not alone in feeling stuck with the painful experiences that show up inside you and have practiced the first steps to becoming more psychologically flexible and living the life you want.

This knowledge is like the foundation of your house, knowledge to understand yourself and manage feelings regarding your mother. The next chapter builds on the foundation. You'll learn how the two styles of narcissism—grandiose and vulnerable—may have showed up in your mother and impacted you.

Chapter 3

Is She a Grandiose or Vulnerable Narcissist?

Narcissism is not a one-size-fits-all phenomenon. Let's say we compare narcissism to ice cream. Ice cream is a cold, creamy dessert. There is vanilla ice cream and even hot sauce–flavored ice cream. Both are ice cream, although very different flavors. Similarly, narcissists are often divided into two main categories: the grandiose narcissistic style and the vulnerable narcissistic style. In this chapter we're going to explore these two styles and their impact.

As you read this information, remember that, like most people with narcissism, your mother likely had, or has, a combination of grandiose and vulnerable traits that wax and wane depending on what is going on in her life. You might see your mother reflected in mostly one category or in a combination of both.

The Main Ingredient: Insecurity

Whether the ice cream flavor is vanilla or hot sauce, the main ingredient is cream. The vanilla or hot sauce gives the ice cream its particular taste and tang. We can think of the grandiose and vulnerable styles as the different flavors of narcissism. The main ingredient they share—the cream—is *insecurity*, the narcissists' sense that, at their core, they're not good enough.

We all have bad days. We snap, perhaps at the people we love most. Perhaps at some innocent bystander, such as the barista brewing our coffee or a dawdling driver. Most of the time, we can step back in these situations and react in a reasonable way, maybe after we have something to eat, call a friend, or get a good night's sleep. Even if we're still upset, we see that the other person wasn't entirely at fault or that it was a challenging situation, such as a crowded coffee shop or a wet road. We can see we overreacted. That's called having self-awareness. And that's what is lacking in people with narcissism. They may be driven by insecurity, but they don't know it. That awareness is sealed off from them, like money stolen and stashed in a secret vault with no clues to crack the safe.

That's one of the things that makes it so hard to be the daughter of a narcissist. Your mother's behavior was repeatedly driven by her hidden store of insecurity and self-doubt. However, in her interactions with you, it looked like you were the problem, the disappointment, the troublemaker, or sometimes, the one she needed to take care of her. Next, let's take a look at how this pattern may have shown up in one of the two primary styles or "flavors" of narcissistic behavior.

The Grandiose Narcissistic Mother

Going back to the ice cream analogy, is your mother like a scoop of hot sauce ice cream? Did she pack a punch with her big personality? If your mother leaned toward the grandiose style, the behaviors and traits in the following list may be familiar to you:

- Appears extremely sure of herself
- Expects special treatment
- Needs to be the center of attention
- Outgoing and confident
- Extremely concerned with appearance and image (her own and yours)
- Relationships are superficial
- May be very successful
- Wants to associate only with successful people
- Brags and name-drops

- Gets angry when spouse or children don't meet expectations

- Can be charming and make people feel special in certain situations

- Cannot tolerate criticism

- Is not bothered by criticism because she doesn't believe any criticism is deserved

- Cannot tolerate letdowns or limits

- Lies to get needs met or cover up failure

In essence, she keeps the spotlight on her, protecting her fragile inner self. She does this through her dominating, my-way-or-the-highway style. She might charm you into doing things her way, but if you want to assert your ideas, you'll see the angry, rejecting side of the grandiose mother. Now let's see how some of the traits and behaviors showed up in a mother-daughter pair, Gabriela and Josefina.

Josefina grew up on Chicago's "Gold Coast." Her parents, Gabriela and Arturo, immigrated to the United States from Mexico with her older brother, Raul, before Josefina's birth. Gabriela and Arturo left their middle-class families in Mexico City to develop the family business. And they succeeded. The family lived in an elegant apartment on the twentieth floor of a high-rise overlooking Lake Michigan. Josefina and Raul attended private schools, took music lessons with elite teachers, and traveled to Europe for vacations.

When Gabriela and Arturo first moved to Chicago, Gabriela felt alone and out of place. Tall and beautiful, she realized her uniqueness could land her a spot in Chicago's high-status circles. Gabriela exaggerated the extent of the family's wealth and connections in Mexico City. Charismatic and determined, she found herself on the boards of art museums and invited to everyone's galas and dinner parties.

Meanwhile, Josefina struggled. While an excellent student, Josefina lacked the social charm of her mother. She found it difficult to fit in at school, where she was one of a handful of girls of color. Once in seventh grade, Josefina confided in her mother how she felt.

"I'm the Mexican girl who doesn't really speak Spanish. I'm not anything!" she said.

"Josefina!" Gabriela said, turning and facing her as she put on her wrap to go out. "Do your homework and stop complaining. You have a fantastic life."

In eighth grade, Josefina asked her mother if she could attend the Catholic high school. Josefina knew there were more Latina girls at that school, and she hoped she could make some friends there.

"Don't be ridiculous!" replied Gabriela. "Do you think I can't choose a school for my daughter? I know better than you do." Josefina regretted her request the moment she made it. Why did she think her mother would ever understand how she felt?

Gabriela gave Josefina the cold shoulder for weeks, seething silently each time Josefina entered a room. Josephina studied more, staying late at school or in her room, keeping as far away from her mother as possible. When Josefina graduated second in her class, Gabriela posed for photos at graduation, beaming, with the biggest bouquet of flowers of any of Josefina's friends. But Josefina knew her mother was embarrassed by her, Gabriela's stiff muscles against Josefina's shoulders her silent giveaway.

As an adult, Josefina's intelligence and background drew her to become an immigration lawyer. Her fierce ability to support her clients often surprised opposing counsel given her quiet demeanor outside of court. Josefina came to therapy because outside of work, she felt riddled with anxiety. "I constantly second-guess myself," she said, sitting straight on the sofa, her feet firmly planted on the floor. "I just bought my first condo. I looked for so long, and I think it's great. My friends love it. But part of me can't help thinking I made a mistake."

Josefina sighs and runs her hands down her long dark hair. "I want to get married and have kids. I'm thirty-two, but I always choose the wrong guy. They're smart and successful but kind of...jerks! Why can't I pick a nice guy?" Josefina asked as she stared out the window, the long legs she inherited from her mother shaking with *nervous energy. "I want to feel confident about myself and my choices. That's it. I want to feel confident being myself."*

Now that you've learned what grandiose narcissism looks like in mothers, please take out your journal and reflect on the following questions. Please remember doing this work is not easy. It's about noticing the emotions and sensations that show up and practicing skills you have learned in previous chapters. Slow down and take a slow, deep belly breath to soothe your nervous system as you proceed through these questions.

- What did it feel like to read the list of behaviors and traits? What emotions showed up for you? Where did you notice those emotions in your body?

- What behaviors and traits could you identify with from the list?

- Does a particular incident or memory come to mind?

The purpose of the next exercise is to help you zoom in on the painful issues that are keeping you stuck. Consider what the problem with your mother has cost you. What will improve when you can handle that problem in new ways? For example, after reading about the grandiose mother, what thoughts, feelings, and memories came up for you? Did you identify any particular challenges in your life as a result? What would you like to be different in your life when you can deal with those challenges differently? The answers to these questions will help you clarify what the problem is.

Practice: Letter to the Problem

In this practice, you'll write a letter to the problem regarding your mother that is getting in the way of your life. It may help to consider Josefina's letter. In therapy, Josefina discussed dating and bringing her mother's voice along in her head, like an unwanted chaperone. She dated men her mother would approve of, with her mother's values and interests. Josefina wanted to listen to her own voice and make choices based on what was important to her. She also learned it's helpful to give a problem a name, so she called this problem her "Stuck Voice." Here is Josefina's letter to the problem.

Dear Stuck Voice,

I've carried you around in my head for a long time, for as long as I can remember. I carried you around in middle school and high school. I took you to college and law school. You never let up criticizing my choices. If you don't directly criticize what I think or do, you have a way of making me second-guess and doubt myself. I wonder what you're thinking I should do.

I know it seems like I've accomplished a lot in my life. I feel good about that. But the way I focus on you and let you have so much power over me takes a big toll. I feel anxious all the time. I doubt myself. I wonder if people really like me. Am I doing the right things in my career? I don't enjoy my life as much as I could because I'm always so worried about what you will think. It's exhausting. I'm missing out on so much, such as just enjoying the moment with friends and appreciating what I have. I realize that I've been dating the kind of guys you would want me to wind up with. I'm not sure who will be right for me. But if I don't stop listening to you, I'll never learn.

I can't stop you from showing up in my head. But I need to pay less attention to you and do what matters to me. I'm sure I'll feel more anxious at first, and I'm willing to feel that way. You'll probably get angry at me too. I'm willing to face all of that because I've given you a free ride long enough. You may show up, but I won't be stuck on you anymore.

Now, I invite you to take out your journal and write your letter to the problem you have identified (Morrow and DuPont Spencer 2018).

If your mother was primarily a grandiose narcissist, the world revolved around her—her experiences, her needs, her ideas. She probably talked a lot about herself. She didn't see you as a separate person with your own interests, opinions, and aptitudes. Your job was to keep her built up, an impossible task. It's no wonder her voice is stuck in your head. How could it not be?

If one of the problems you perceive is stuck thoughts about your mother, here is another practice that may help. For Josefina, the first step in accomplishing her goal of not listening to her stuck voice was to *notice* when she heard it and then gently let go of it. She practiced that through mindfulness and a practice known as Floating Leaves on a Moving Stream, created by Steven C. Hayes (2005), one of the creators of ACT.

Practice: Leaves on a Stream

You can read the script below and practice on your own, or you can go to http://www.newharbinger.com/50096 to listen to a recording of it.

1. Sit in a comfortable position and either close your eyes or rest them gently on a fixed spot in the room.

2. Visualize yourself sitting beside a gently flowing stream with leaves floating along the surface of the water. *Pause for ten seconds.*

3. For the next few minutes, take each thought that enters your mind and place it on a leaf...let it float by. Do this with each thought—pleasurable, painful, or neutral. Even if you have joyous or enthusiastic thoughts, place them on a leaf and let them float by.

4. If your thoughts momentarily stop, continue to watch the stream. Sooner or later, your thoughts will start up again. *Pause for twenty seconds.*

5. Allow the stream to flow at its own pace. Don't try to speed it up and rush your thoughts along. You're not trying to rush the leaves along or "get rid" of your thoughts. You are allowing them to come and go at their own pace.

6. If your mind says, "This is dumb," "I'm bored," or "I'm not doing this right," place *those thoughts* on leaves too and let them pass. *Pause for twenty seconds.*

7. If a leaf gets stuck, allow it to hang around until it's ready to float by. If the thought comes up again, watch it float by another time. *Pause for twenty seconds.*

8. If a difficult or painful feeling arises, simply acknowledge it. Say to yourself, "I notice myself having a feeling of boredom, impatience, frustration," or whatever the feeling is. Place those thoughts on leaves and allow them to float along.

9. From time to time, your thoughts may hook you and distract you from being fully present in this exercise. This is *normal*. As soon as you realize that you have become sidetracked, gently bring your attention back to the visualization exercise.

As you practice, you'll notice when your mother's voice shows up (and it will!). This helps you recognize what matters to you—your values—so you can do something different. In acceptance and commitment therapy, this is known as *committed action*. Next, we'll look at the quieter version of the narcissistic mother, the vulnerable narcissistic mother.

The Vulnerable Narcissistic Mother

This type of narcissistic mother is quieter and harder to identify than the grandiose narcissistic mother. She's not as well-known. She's, well, the vanilla to the "hot sauce" grandiose version. She is sometimes called the "fragile narcissist" because she seems unsure of herself, in contrast to the grandiose narcissist.

If you had a vulnerable narcissistic mother, she may seem depressed and unhappy with her life. On the surface, she may have appeared to think little of herself and at the same time had the ability to demand a great deal of others. Like the grandiose mother, she was unaware of her feelings, limiting her ability to understand yours. She may have relied on you to take care of her, medically, financially, or emotionally. You may have been her confidante, the one she looked to to solve her problems.

If your mother leaned toward the vulnerable style, the behaviors and traits in the following list may be familiar to you. You may also notice overlap with the list for the grandiose mother.

- Feels unsure of herself, or "less than" other people

- Struggles with depression or anxiety

- Is envious of others

- Lacks independence

- Has difficulty with focus in work, leisure interests, and maintaining friendships

- Is easily hurt by (perceived) criticism

- Has limited social skills, may appear anxious or even "odd" in social situations

How does she keep the spotlight on her, to protect her fragile inner self? Through her neediness and adeptness at getting you to feel guilty, making you feel responsible for things that are not your job to be responsible for. If you try to assert yourself or set limits, she'll show her mean side and that in fact, she's capable of standing up for herself. Now, let's see how some of the traits and behaviors showed up in a mother-daughter pair, Sharon and Ilana.

Ilana's mother, Sharon, worked hard to raise Ilana on her own. Ilana never knew her father. Sharon said they had a brief relationship. When she found out she was pregnant, she knew she wanted to keep the baby, even though girls from middle-class families didn't do that. Ilana appreciated that her mother went to work every day as an administrative assistant at an advertising agency. Sharon persisted even though her boss made passes at her, her friend got promoted instead of Sharon, and the commute exhausted her.

Ilana tried hard to make her mother's life easier. Ilana listened to Sharon's problems and sensed when her mother had a bad day as soon as Sharon walked in the door. Starting in fifth grade, Ilana had dinner ready for her mother when she came home from work. She got perfect grades and decided to forgo after-school activities so she could take care of things at home. That was fine with Sharon.

Occasionally, before Sharon came home from work, Ilana would spend the afternoon at her friend Caroline's house, whose mother, Stacy, was an elementary school aide. Stacy sat at the kitchen table with Ilana and Caroline and asked them about their days. Stacy remembered how hard middle school was, trying to fit in, and how the "popular girls" got all the attention. Ilana and Caroline sat on the couch and watched TV or did their homework at the kitchen table while Stacy made dinner or helped Caroline's younger brother with his homework. Until she met Caroline, Ilana never knew a family could feel like this way: comfortable, relaxed, and just "normal." In eighth grade, Ilana signed up for the school trip to Washington, DC, and talked about it all year. A couple of days before the trip, Sharon came down with the flu.

"Maybe I shouldn't go to Washington," Ilana tentatively offered Sharon, allowing herself to hope, for once, that Sharon would be okay on her own.

"Maybe you're right," said Sharon. "Thanks, honey. I don't know what I'd without you. Anyway, it's such a long bus ride. You'd probably hate it."

In some ways, the mother who has primarily vulnerable traits is the most confusing to her daughter. Like Sharon, she may struggle to fully care for herself and her daughter. She may be critical and controlling while competently caring for her everyday needs. She might also be self-doubting, sensitive to criticism, and envious, even of—or especially of—her own daughter. Like her grandiose counterpart, her feelings take over any interaction without her being able to see the repercussions. Let's look at how this played out for Ilana as an adult.

At twenty-three, Ilana met her husband, Dave, during her first year teaching elementary school when Dave, a car mechanic, repaired her Honda Civic. They married a year later, and their daughter, Mariah, soon followed.

Ilana, now forty, is a teacher and mother to Mariah, age fourteen, and Corinna, age thirteen. Ilana came to therapy because she felt overwhelmed working, doing the housework, and raising two teenage daughters. Until now, it's been...manageable. Now her two girls roll their eyes at her and stomp around the house. Ilana feels frustrated and irritated at them, and then guilty for feeling that way.

Sharon, now retired, lives in the other half of their two-family home. Ilana does her grocery shopping, even though Sharon drives and is physically fit. Sharon finds the supermarket "too crazy." When Corinna and Mariah were younger, Ilana would occasionally ask Sharon to pick the girls up from the bus stop in the afternoon if she had a late meeting after school or an appointment. Sharon was always busy or "just not up to it."

As room mother, Girl Scout leader, and Sunday school teacher, Ilana prides herself on remaining calm and together. No one can know she feels so alone and out of control. She doesn't have any close friends. She's always been too busy to get to know anyone.

Many daughters of vulnerable narcissistic mothers, like Ilana, grow up trying to do everything right. They know something isn't right at home, in their family—but what? It's so hard to put a finger on. Maybe it will help to do everything just right. Now that you've learned what vulnerable narcissism looks like in mothers, please take out your journal and reflect on the following questions:

- What did it feel like to read the list of behaviors and traits? What emotions showed up for you? Where did you notice those emotions in your body?

- What behaviors and traits could you identify with from the list?

- Does a particular incident or memory come to mind?

Ilana realized that the more she tried to do everything and keep everything under control, the worse she felt. For Ilana, trying to do everything was the only way she knew to feel like herself and that things would be okay. She didn't know any other way that people, even her own family, could love her, or that the world wouldn't fall apart. The following practice helped Ilana recognize the cost of holding onto needing to take care of everything. See what happens when you try it with an issue you are struggling with. If you'd like to listen to this practice, you can find the recording at http://www.newharbinger.com/50096.

Practice: Holding a Pen

Imagine a particular problem that you've been struggling with, such as worrying you're going to get laid off, the ten pounds you can't lose, or how your mother will act at your child's graduation party.

1. Pick up a pen, and let it rest on the outstretched palm of one of your hands.

2. Squeeze the pen as hard as you have been working on the problem.

3. Really concentrate on all the time and energy and emotion you have put into that problem. Continue to squeeze the pen as hard as the effort you've been putting into that problem.

4. Notice what you feel in your hand—tension, discomfort, and so forth.

5. Think of a scale of 1 to 10, with 10 being the tightest. Using that scale, rate how hard you are squeezing the pen.

6. Now, still holding onto the pen, bring the amount of tightness down by half. Note what that feels like and how it feels different from before.

7. Now, see if you can bring it down it little more so you are holding the pen just enough to keep it in your hand without dropping it.

8. Notice what if feels like to hold the pen just that much. Just enough to hold onto to the pen. Not too much, not too little. How does it feel to hold the pen that way? What does that tell you about the problem you've identified? Could you imagine holding onto the problem more lightly, with less force, without dropping it altogether? What would that look like for you? How would that make a difference in your life?

The Holding a Pen exercise helped Ilana notice that she could practice letting go of doing so much, at the expense of herself, step by step, even if she wasn't fully ready to. It helped Ilana set a goal of noticing when she heard the voice in her head telling her that she wasn't doing enough. She noticed what that felt like in her body and how it impacted her behavior. She took the time to pause, even for a moment, to step back from those thoughts, emotions, or urges and let go, to "hold the pen" less tightly. She noticed how it made a difference for her.

For example, Ilana decided to notice times during the week when her husband helped out around the house and her daughters did things that showed that they were becoming more independent. Just like she didn't have to do everything, she didn't have to make every change happen either. She kept a log on her phone and gave herself small rewards when she didn't jump in to do things her family members could do for themselves. After a few months, Ilana started to feel like she had more free time, and she joined a book group in her neighborhood. She began to feel less alone and isolated.

In this chapter, you learned that mothers with narcissistic traits and behaviors fall into primary, although overlapping, categories: grandiose and vulnerable. You stepped back to figure out how these experiences impacted you. You learned that with practice, little by little, you can loosen the grip on your anxiety and get unstuck from problems related to your relationship to your mother no matter what happens with her.

In the next chapter, we'll look at a common experience of daughters—the feeling that they can't trust themselves, the constant second-guessing, pervasive feelings of guilt, anger, and shame. Where does that come from? How can it get better? Let's find out.

Chapter 4

Identifying Gaslighting and Lack of Empathy

In this chapter you'll learn about two common patterns in narcissistic mothers: gaslighting and lack of or compromised empathy. You'll learn how these patterns impacted you and how you can recover from them. Like gas itself, when someone gaslights you, it's invisible. You don't know it's there until it overpowers you. Even then, you might not know where it's coming from. If you experienced gaslighting, it may have made you doubt yourself. It may have made you feel crazy. The term "gaslighting" comes from a 1938 play (also a 1944 movie) *Gas Light*, in which a husband sets out to drive his wife "crazy" so he can get his hands on her money. For example, he unexpectedly turns the lights (which are powered by gas) on and off. When she wonders why it's dark in the house, he tells her it's not dark. There must be something wrong with her. Gaslighting's calling cards and, as it happens, the first three letters of the term, are guilt, anger, and shame.

Your mother might gaslight you deliberately, or it could be behavior that occurs out of her awareness. Whatever the process, you're left with the fundamental questions: What's wrong with me? Can I trust my own thoughts, feelings, and views of the world? Can I trust other people? Here are the nine styles of gaslighting.

The minimizer. The minimizer dismisses and rejects your feelings. She says things such as: "You're so sensitive." "You're blowing this out of proportion." "Just put this behind you."

You learn to ignore your emotions and often don't know what you are feeling. You doubt your thoughts, feelings, and decisions, constantly hearing that "critical" or "doubting" voice in your head.

The woe-is-me-er. The woe-is-me-er can always top her daughter's feelings, needs, or problems with her own. She says things such as: "I'm doing the best I can." "You think you've had a hard day? You should hear about my day!" "At least you can take an antibiotic. For me, there's no cure. Just ongoing pain."

You learn to feel guilty, even ashamed about your emotions, about wanting things, about taking care of your own needs. You take care of others before yourself but also feel frustrated, overwhelmed, and angry. You don't learn to trust your own pain, whether emotional or physical. You don't listen to your emotional or physical signals.

The threat-thrower. The threat-thrower keeps her daughter off-balance by intimidation and attacking her sense of security. She says things such as: "Maybe we shouldn't see each other anymore." "Maybe I won't bring your grandmother to your wedding." "I don't need to keep you in the will."

You learn that it is difficult to trust people. You may have difficulty forming close relationships with others and tend to question other people's intentions or goodwill. It's hard to feel you can be loved unconditionally; you feel you need to earn the love of those in your life.

The subject-changer. The subject-changer avoids responsibility for her behavior by ignoring direct questions, as if she has a deadly allergy to them. A conversation with her goes like this:

Daughter: Mom, from now on I need you to call before you come over. It's not okay just to stop by.

Mom: Have you talked to your brother lately? I think he's on vacation.

Daughter: Rick's company might be having layoffs. I don't know what we'll do if he gets laid off again.

Mom: Oh, it's 5:00 p.m. I have to leave for tennis.

Daughter: Mom! Did you hear what I just said?

Mom: You know my schedule. I always leave for tennis at five on Thursdays.

You don't feel your points are valid because you never get to complete your thoughts. You don't feel safe talking about your emotions and experiences because you don't get to fully process what you are thinking and feeling. Everything is cut off midstream.

You learn to second-guess yourself and question your own judgment, like the daughter of the minimizer and the daughter of the subject-changer. You have difficulty trusting others and letting others get to know you.

The put-downer. The put-downer gains control over her daughter and causes her to doubt herself by chipping away at her self-esteem with criticism and insults. She says things such as: "You're so selfish." "You've always given us such a hard time. Not like your sister." "You should have…" "Why didn't you…"

You learn to doubt yourself and are highly self-critical. It feels like nothing you do is ever good enough. You feel a deep sense of unworthiness and hold yourself back from important parts of life, friendships, intimate relationships, education, or work. You don't learn to stand up for yourself. You struggle with anxiety and the critical voice in your head.

The cross-examiner. The cross-examiner interrogates her daughter as if there is a mother-daughter-expectations contract and the daughter has violated it. She says things such as: "I thought you said you had to stay home this weekend to do spring cleaning. But when I called, Mark told me you were at yoga." "You didn't tell me you invited Barbara to your bridal shower."

You learn to hide yourself from others, to isolate, maybe to even be secretive. You feel micromanaged, angry, and frustrated, as if you've broken a rule you never agreed to in the first place. You feel overwhelmed, not sure what to focus on, or questioning yourself. *Who said you can't go to yoga? What's the problem with Barbara?*

The defender. The defender bolsters her version of reality with "facts" and leaves no room for debate. She says things such as: "I've always been a good mother. Everyone says so. You are just ungrateful." "I have lot of friends. Everyone likes me." "I'm a very kind person. I chair the hospital gala every year." "I only had good intentions. I thought you would appreciate if Aunt Sally knew you were going through in-vitro."

You learn to doubt your thoughts, feelings, and perceptions. You learn to become very sensitive. Alternatively, you can become defensive and argumentative yourself, skills learned in the heat of battle that sometimes serve you well and sometimes don't.

The denier. The denier simply changes the facts of things she said or did to be consistent with the image she wants to present or the result she currently wants. The denier might say things such as: "That never happened." "I don't remember that." "I came to all your basketball games when you were in high school." "I don't know what you're talking about!"

You learn to have difficulty trusting others. You second-guess yourself and look to others for validation of your opinions. You may have a hard time making decisions because you can't trust your judgment or inner voice. You feel angry at your mother and then question that emotion; maybe you wonder if there is something wrong with you.

The accounter. The accounter keeps track of who does what for her and when. She says things such as: "Your brother calls me every night. I'm lucky you can squeeze in a call on the weekend." "When I stayed with your cousin, she always paid for dinner when we went out."

You learn to doubt your self-worth. Maybe you push yourself too hard, trying to be perfect in other parts of your life. Maybe you've given up on yourself. You hear worry in your head all the time, wondering if you're doing the right thing.

Your mother might engage in any of these styles. As we discussed previously, your mother struggles with knowing who she is and what she wants from life, having close relationships, and handling her own emotions. These critical adult skills fluctuate depending on what's going on in her life: Does she feel successful? Taken care of? That she's getting enough attention? Also, how is she perceiving her own pain? How rejected does she feel because you said you'd be home cleaning but in fact, you went to yoga? She sees the world from her own point of view and can't see it any other way. All these factors impact her tendency to gaslight and in what way. This is a good time to take out your journal and reflect on what you just read.

- What thoughts, emotions, physical sensations, or urges showed up for you as you read about gaslighting?

- Did your mother engage in any gaslighting behaviors? If so, which ones?

- Does a particular incident come to mind? Do you remember how it made you feel or think about yourself or others?

Sarah walks in the door, drops her backpack in the front hall, and heads to the kitchen for a snack. She has an hour to chill out from ninth grade before her after-school babysitting job. Just as Sarah opens the refrigerator, Roberta, her mother, grabs her shoulder.

"What's going on with you?" Roberta demands.

"I'm getting a snack," Sarah replies, flustered.

"I mean at school. I got a call from your math teacher today. She told me you got Ds on your last two tests. And you haven't been turning in all your homework. I had no idea. I was so embarrassed."

"I'm sorry, Mom. We've been doing this stuff that's really hard."

"That's no excuse. You know Dad and I always tell you to ask for help. That's what your teachers are for. Why do you think we live in

this expensive school district? How does it make me look that I don't know what's going on with my own daughter? Sometimes I think you're just plain lazy." Roberta stomps out of the kitchen.

Sarah's hand slides off the refrigerator handle, her appetite now an anxious pit of shame in her stomach. She knows she should have gone for help and told her parents the trouble she was having with math. But Sarah didn't want to face...this. This feeling that somehow the worst thing is disappointing her mother. Worse than having a bad grade in math. Sometimes Sarah thinks that if she ignores problems, they will just go away. Well...screw her! They're her grades! Maybe she won't go to college. Then she won't have to care about math anymore.

That evening, after Sarah returns from babysitting, her parents sit her down on the sofa to talk about the math situation. Sarah's father, Gerry, reaches for Sarah's hand. "Honey, Mom told me what a hard time you're having with math right now. She said she already told you it's not a problem, and we're going to get you a tutor, okay? Mom and I just want to help." Roberta doesn't acknowledge her unkind words from earlier, the blowout at the refrigerator. Roberta smiles sweetly at Sarah.

"Okay," says Sarah. She goes back to her room and curls up on her bed, confused and sad. There must be something wrong with her because she doesn't feel better now. Her parents are getting her a tutor. Maybe she won't fail math. She'll just keep her feelings to herself, like she always does. That's the only way to survive, like a ghost in her own house. Where is the mother who was yelling at her just hours earlier? It's like that whole blowup never happened, and now Sarah is dealing with a different mother, the supportive, caring mother who is getting her a tutor. Sarah wonders if there's something wrong with her because she felt so upset before. Maybe she's the crazy one.

As an adult, Sarah knocks on her mother's door and checks her watch again. She's sure she has the time and date correct to drive her mother, Roberta, to her yearly mammogram. Roberta could drive herself, but any medical procedure makes Roberta so anxious that she insists that Sarah take her. Sarah took time off work, moving around her physical therapy patients to the weekend to accommodate this *appointment. So where is Roberta? Finally, Sarah calls Roberta, and she answers immediately.*

"I'm with Linda. She's driving me. You never got back to me, so I asked her to take me," Roberta states crisply.

"Mom, we talked about this on Monday. I told you I'd pick you up at ten."

"Well, I don't remember that," Roberta replies. "You'd said you'd try. You're not very reliable, so I asked Linda. We're here now. I have to go." Roberta hangs up on Sarah, who stands stunned on the steps of her mother's home.

For a few moments, Sarah's body feels frozen. What just happened? She recalls talking to her mother on Monday, confirming the plans. Is she losing her mind? She keeps losing her keys. Maybe there is something wrong with her mind. Or maybe she's unreliable like Roberta said. Her mother always knows just how to hurt her. Linda probably thinks she's a terrible daughter! And now she's working on Saturday for no reason, instead of going hiking with her friends. Roberta doesn't care about her schedule one bit. When will this end?

These encounters with her mother carry over into other relationships, especially when Sarah thinks she might be falling in love. A year after her last breakup, she met Caroline at a party. They've been dating for four months, and it's going, well…great. Sarah can't believe how lucky she feels. Except now they're planning their first (long) weekend away. Caroline, an avid skier, wants to head to the slopes. She knows it shouldn't matter, but Sarah is finding it so difficult to tell Caroline that the weekend she has in mind isn't in her budget. Sarah feels ashamed and small. What will Caroline think when she finds out that Sarah is still paying off her grad school loans?

Caroline is wonderful, yes. Warm and nonjudgmental. Still, Sarah finds it hard to imagine that someone could accept her as she is or not twist her words around. What if Caroline thinks she misrepresented herself somehow? She doesn't know what to do, so Sarah puts off planning the weekend, coming up with excuses. Now she's worried that Caroline will think she isn't serious about her or doesn't want to go away with her.

Sarah's story illustrates gaslighting behavior patterns and how a daughter can be impacted in terms of her self-worth throughout her life. Let's look more closely at the three emotions that often result from gaslighting: guilt, anger, and shame.

Guilt

Guilt is the feeling that we've done something wrong, something that goes against our moral compass. Guilt often gets a bad rap because we often feel guilty when we shouldn't. We feel guilty when we've disappointed *someone else*, not ourselves. This is easy to do when you're the daughter of a narcissistic mother. However, we need guilt. We don't want to get rid of this emotion. Without it, we'd have no sense of right or wrong. For example, if you hit a car in a parking lot, dent the bumper, and drive away without leaving a note, you might consider whether that should tug at your conscience. We don't need guilt for:

- feeling what we feel

- thinking what we think

- making our own choices in life

Are you the daughter of a woe-is-me-er or a cross-examiner? If so, you may have grown up with the feeling that you were always, somehow, doing something wrong, even though you were making your own decisions and, well, growing up. That feeling may have been squashed down and unacknowledged, but it lingers. As Marc Brackett (2019) says in his book *Permission to Feel*, "Hurt feelings don't vanish on their own. They don't heal themselves. If we don't express our emotions, they pile up like a debt that will eventually come due" (13).

Anger

Anger, like guilt, is an essential emotion, but one that's often difficult to handle, especially for women and especially for daughters of narcissistic mothers. Anger serves one main purpose: it alerts us that our rights have been violated, that we feel we've been treated unfairly in some way. Are you the daughter of a denier or an accounter? You may have felt enraged when your mother simply changed the facts of what was happening or when she kept tabs on what you do for her (and you always come up short). But there's no room for you to express your feelings or set the record straight.

Shame

Shame is one of the most complicated and painful human emotions, and it becomes deeply embedded in our sense of self (Ashley 2020). It's also a gateway to other emotions, such as depression and anxiety. Unlike guilt and anger, which are necessary emotions, shame never serves us well. Shame is the feeling of being fundamentally flawed, fraudulent, or unlovable.

Are you the daughter of a minimizer or threat-thrower? You may have learned that your feelings were wrong or inappropriate or that you would be rejected for them. You may have learned that *you* were wrong for having them. These forms of gaslighting are breeding grounds for shame.

Guilt, anger, and shame are fueled by gaslighting behavior. What do all the strategies have in common? The common thread is a lack of empathy, a mother's compromised ability to understand and show compassion for her daughter's feelings and what she needs in life. Let's look at the role of empathy in narcissistic mothers.

Do Narcissists Feel Empathy?

Empathy is the capacity to understand others' emotions or perspectives, to put yourself in their shoes as best you can, even if you've never walked in them. It seems that narcissism and empathy go together like oil and water: they just don't mix. However, the mental health profession has sharpened its understanding of the concept of empathy in general and how it works in narcissism. Empathy can be broken down into two types: cognitive and emotional.

Cognitive Empathy

Cognitive empathy is the ability to understand what someone is thinking and feeling, or the ability to see things from someone else's perspective without really understanding the other person's emotions inside. This is a tricky distinction. It's sort of like logical empathy, or being able to say the right words without true feeling behind them.

For example, when Riley learned about cognitive empathy, she reported: "My mother could say the right things when I was upset, but somehow I never felt comforted. There was no warmth to her words. Now I understand why I never felt better. I thought there was something wrong with me."

Emotional Empathy

Emotional empathy is the ability to feel what someone is feeling (what we normally think of when we think about empathy). Healthy empathy requires the capacity to understand someone else's feelings and experiences from an appropriate distance without getting overwhelmed by the other person's emotions. When someone gets overwhelmed by the other's emotions, they lose their ability to listen or help as needed.

With a narcissistic mother, her "empathy" is her own emotions gone overboard, drowning out her daughter's needs. Mary Sue recalls that when she didn't get the lead in the school play, her mother was "heartbroken for her," crying all weekend. Mary Sue was disappointed, but her mother's "empathy" turned a disappointment into a disaster, an insurmountable roadblock to future roles instead of a bump in the road. Her mother's reaction overshadowed Mary Sue's own experience in not getting the role, making it all about her mother's overwhelmed emotional state.

Next, let's look at what makes it difficult for your mother to experience and show empathy for you. In order to feel and display empathy for your emotions, your mother needs to first step back and identify what she is feeling and handle her own emotions. As we know, people with narcissism experience a constellation of traits that impede their ability do that. For example, when someone's first reaction is to blame someone else in a misunderstanding, it will be very difficult for her to step back, see things from the other person's point of view, and then understand her feelings about the situation. Your mother may have had some or all of the following traits, which would have made it difficult for her to be empathetic to your feelings (Russ et al., 2008):

- Fear of rejection and abandonment

- Feeling misunderstood

- Extreme reactions to perceived slights or criticisms

- Tendency for depression or anxiety

- Tendency for anger or hostility

- Tendency to blame others

- Tendency to get into power struggles with others

Your mother's difficulties with empathy likely emerged from her own upbringing. We'll take a look at that next.

How Did She Get This Way?

There's an old saying in psychology: Are psychological challenges caused by nature or nurture? Answer: Both. Likewise, your mother's narcissism is due to a complex mix of her innate temperament and genetics, her family situation and upbringing, the society and culture she grew up in, and the significant events that shaped her childhood. Your mother was likely raised in one of three types of families, which contributed to her adult personality style (Behary 2013).

First, your mother may have been overindulged as a child or teen. Perhaps her parents set few rules, limits, or consequences. A 2015 study found that narcissism in children is cultivated when parents "overvalue" them—that is, believe their children are more special and entitled than others (Brummelman et al. 2015).

Second, she may have had parents who did everything for her: parents who didn't want her to struggle at all or feel any of the pain that goes along with growing up. As such, your mother never learned to cope with difficult emotions or take care of herself. As an adult, like the overvalued mother, she expects others to take care of her.

Finally, your mother may have been raised in a family in which she was loved for what she did, rather than for who she was. She learned she must perform perfectly to please her parents. Since life was a performance, it was difficult for her to develop a sense of who she is, how she feels, or what she wants. As an adult, your mother continues to perform, making it very difficult to create authentic relationships with other people.

Now that we've looked at gaslighting—what it is and where it comes from—let's explore how to deal with its impact.

Lowering the GAS: Best Steps

Like many daughters of narcissistic mothers, you may have worked hard at acceptance. You may have told yourself regularly: "I know she's narcissistic. She's not going to change." However, as one daughter, Marlene, said: "I accept that my mother is narcissistic. So why don't I feel better?" Acceptance seems like it should help, that it should somehow create feelings of peace and well-being. And yet for many women it doesn't. There's nothing wrong per se with trying to accept a narcissistic mother. So why doesn't it work better?

That's where acceptance and commitment therapy (ACT) comes in. ACT focuses on helping you accept what goes on inside of you (your feelings, thoughts, urges, and memories about Mom) instead of what goes on outside of you (Mom's behavior). According to ACT, it's human nature to avoid distressing thoughts, emotions, memories, urges, and physical sensations. However, the more you try to get rid of all that—everything unwanted that shows up inside, that other people can't see—the more it sticks around (Hayes, Strosahl, and Wilson, 2012).

Did you notice the word "avoid"? We do many things to avoid our painful inner experiences. Remember Sarah from the beginning of this chapter? Sarah felt guilty and angry when her mother demanded Sarah take her to appointments with no regard to Sarah's schedule. To make matters worse, she felt ashamed for feeling this way, like a bad daughter. So she did, without question, what her mother asked. This behavior helped Sarah avoid her feelings of guilt and anger, feelings that seemed unbearable. This made sense for Sarah. But unfortunately, those feelings showed up anyway. She felt guilty, angry, and ashamed. Then she felt frustrated and inadequate because she was trying so hard to cope. Sarah's first step toward healing was learning that she wasn't inadequate, a failure, or a bad daughter. It wasn't that she was not accepting of her mother. She needed new strategies for the problem.

For Sarah, an important step for change was accepting her thoughts and feelings. She willingly allowed herself to have them. This might sound crazy. Who would want to feel that stuff on purpose? And yet there is a clear purpose: to live the life you want and to make the choices you want to make based on your values. Learning to accept what you feel inside takes practice. Here's a practice based on a metaphor, which helped Sarah. The quicksand metaphor was created by Steven C. Hayes, PhD, one of the creators of ACT.

Practice: The Quicksand Metaphor

Imagine you are walking in a beautiful place, perhaps a jungle or rainforest. You're having a lovely time, enjoying the sights and scents around you. Suddenly, out of nowhere, you feel yourself sucked down. You realize you've stepped into quicksand. Sink, sink, sink. You're flailing around. You want to get out of there fast. So you start peddling your legs and pulling your arms, anything to get out of the quicksand. Except you find you're sinking farther, faster. The more you try to get out, the more the quicksand sucks you back in.

Then, you remember what you read about quicksand. The more you fight it, the more it sucks you back in. So even though your heart is pounding and every part of you wants to fight your way out, you pause. You stretch out your body on top of the quicksand. You allow your body to make contact with it. You allow yourself to float on top of the quicksand; you just allow yourself to be there and stop fighting it and struggling with it. Another part of you shouts "No! Keep scrambling! This won't work!" But you let those thoughts go by. And soon you can roll off the quicksand.

It's human nature to struggle when we feel trapped. We keep doing the things we know don't work until we realize that we can free ourselves by doing something else.

Below is a list of questions to help you understand how you struggle in the "quicksand." This is a good time to write in your journal.

- Think of a situation that you are struggling with now, whether related to your mother or not. Describe it briefly in your journal.
- What thoughts, emotions, memories, urges, and physical sensations (inner experiences) are associated with this struggle?
- What actions have you been taking to avoid having contact with your inner experiences?
- How are those actions helping you?
- How are those actions hurting you?

This practice is your first step in understanding the power of making room for your thoughts and feelings. You learned about the difference between accepting your thoughts and feelings and accepting situations in life.

Cognitive Defusion

It's important to realize that we cannot help the feelings, thoughts, memories, or urges that show up inside us. You can, however, practice different ways to respond to them. One way is to observe your thoughts objectively, without letting them hijack you emotionally. In ACT, this process is called "defusion." Defusion means putting some space between yourself and your thoughts so they don't run your life. Often when you're overwhelmed by your thoughts, it seems like that there's no escape because your thoughts are all-encompassing. You're not alone in that experience! As Pema Chödrön (2018) writes in *Comfortable with Uncertainty*, "Trying to find the moment when one thought becomes another is like trying to find the moment when boiling water turns into steam" (9). There is another way to move back from your thoughts, also known as unhooking (Harris 2019).

Imagine your mind is like any other source of information that you hear but don't take seriously or even pay attention to. That source of information may be hard or impossible to tune out, but that doesn't mean you accept what it says. What is that source for you? The news station your father-in-law loves? Your neighbor's complaining about the cost of the new high school? You probably have strategies to handle these situations. Perhaps you think about something else more pleasant. Perhaps you say: "Well, it's nice talking to you. Gotta run!" Maybe you say: "No kidding. I didn't know that," or "Interesting."

Now, imagine talking to your mind this way! When it starts to recite its usual litany of annoying information, tell it: "No kidding," or "Interesting!"

What else could you say to "unhook" your mind from your thoughts? How will this help you?

In this chapter you learned what gaslighting is, how your mother may have used it, how it impacted you, and skills to handle the common feelings of guilt, anger, and shame that linger for adult daughters. You learned how your mother's unmet needs impacted her ability to provide you with true empathy. In the next chapter, we'll focus on your anxious thought patterns and how you can take control.

Chapter 5

Disrupt Your Anxious Thought Patterns

Some people can let go of negative thoughts when they want to, just like they toss out junk mail, never to think of it again. Their motto is "Why worry?" If you're like most daughters of narcissistic mothers, it's unlikely that's your style. It's more likely that as you go about your day, you're having a nonstop conversation in your mind, with yourself. And it's not a kind, supportive conversation. Oh no.

If people could listen in, they'd hear you beating yourself up about a past mistake. Or maybe the eavesdroppers to your inner monologues would hear you agonizing over whether you'll get promoted at your job. Your boss seems happy with your work. But what if you get passed over? You'll have wasted your time and feel like a loser. Perhaps you're having a conversation in your mind with someone else, replaying what you said and what you think should have said instead. Maybe you're replaying the disagreement you had last month with your best friend, regretting your angry words, until you're so sad you wonder why anyone would be your friend in the first place.

You wish you could live, just a little, in the here and now, appreciate the moment, and not be so caught up in your head. You wish, for once, that you didn't go over everything repeatedly, as if you could change the past or control the future if you worried about it enough. But living in the moment and letting go of anxious thoughts have never been your way. At the very least, you'd love to turn off the tape in your brain for a little bit and listen to something else.

The worst part is this negative thinking feels like it's your fault, a character flaw, a weakness. It's a double whammy of shame and self-blame.

First, you blame yourself for all the things you did or didn't do. Then, you blame yourself because you can't stop thinking about them. In the next section, you'll learn more about this type of thinking. You'll learn why it may show up more frequently in daughters of narcissistic mothers. Then, you'll learn what you can do about it.

Your (Too) Busy Brain

First, let's talk about the style of thinking you just read about. Mental health professionals have a term for it: "repetitive negative thinking," or RNT. This is an umbrella term that captures multiple types of negative thinking patterns. There's *worry*, which is negative thoughts and predictions about the future. There's *rumination*, which is negative thoughts and dwelling on the past. Finally, there are negative thoughts about what's happening in the here and now (Kertz et al. 2015).

These thought patterns play a role in a number of mental health issues, particularly anxiety disorders, depression, and sleep problems. People with social anxiety, generalized anxiety, obsessive compulsive disorder, and post-traumatic stress disorder, among other issues, report struggles with RNT (Monteregge et al. 2020). In addition, RNT has a negative impact on our immune and cardiovascular systems, memory, and stress levels.

It's possible that you struggle with issues related to being the daughter of a narcissistic mother *and* you have a common mental health problem, such as an anxiety disorder, depression, or trauma-related disorder. It's beyond the scope of this book to describe all of these mental health conditions. *However, if you think you might be struggling with one of these mental health problems, please seek an evaluation and therapy from a qualified professional.*

RNT and Daughters of Narcissistic Mothers

There's limited formal psychological research on the impact of narcissistic parents on their children (Hart et al. 2017). However, things are slowly changing. Some studies shed light, even if it's indirect, on why you struggle with RNT and the frustration, self-blame, and shame that can go along with it. One study found that young adults with narcissistic parents were more likely to report experiencing depression and anxiety than were the young adults in the study whose parents were not narcissistic (Dentale et al. 2015). Why is this important? Remember that RNT is common in people who experience depression and anxiety (Kertz et al. 2015).

Another study found that narcissistic parents were less likely to treat their children with empathy. Narcissistic parents were less likely to engage in what's known as *authoritative parenting* (Hart et al. 2017). Authoritative parents are warm and develop close relationships with their children. Authoritative parents listen to their children's point of view and respect their feelings while at the same time set appropriate limits. This type of parenting has long been considered by the mental health profession to raise children who grow up to be self-confident, flexible, independent, and assertive, characteristics that likely serve as a buffer from anxiety, depression, and RNT. Next, let's look at Michelle's story and how RNT impacted her life.

> Michelle came to therapy two months before her thirteen-year-old son Alex's bar mitzvah. "I'm not worried about Alex," she confided. "He's doing fine preparing for the service. It's me. I can't stop worrying that something will go wrong. What if Alex gets sick? What if none of his friends show up?"
>
> Michelle explained that her mom-friends worried about this occasion, but not like her. Michelle felt anxious and unsure of herself. She wanted to guarantee that each guest was perfectly pleased and that the whole day went off without a hitch. Worst of all, she felt her anxiety was starting to rub off on Alex.
>
> Michelle's parents divorced when she was in middle school. Her father remarried when she was in high school. Her mother, Rochelle, complained about Michelle's father and his second wife on a regular basis. Michelle tried her best to quietly listen and comfort her mother. Michelle often felt like the object of Rochelle's jealousy and criticism, although Rochelle would never have seen it that way. You went out to lunch with her? Did the two of you actually eat? She's practically anorexic.

Michelle admitted that much of her time was still spent worrying about her mother's well-being and behavior and what Michelle should do to make her happy. Although it had been decades since the marriage ended, her mother's anger had not abated. Now that the bar mitzvah was approaching, Michelle felt consumed by anxious thoughts. How would her mother act at the bar mitzvah? Would she complain to everyone about Michelle's father? Tell everyone about her problems?

For once, Michelle wanted to enjoy herself and this milestone in her family's life. She didn't want her mother to be the focus of her attention. Michelle felt stuck and overwhelmed. She felt responsible for her mother's happiness, as she had since middle school, and then felt guilty when she resented feeling responsible. It was a vicious cycle. Plus, here she was—a grown woman with a family of her own. She's tired of living in her head and not living her life. It would be so, well, embarrassing if anyone knew how much room her mother still took up in her head.

Michelle struggles with RNT, and it's not surprising. Michelle discovered that her mother had key traits of narcissism, particularly self-centeredness and lack of empathy. Remember the grandiose and vulnerable narcissistic styles from chapter 3? Rochelle, like many people with narcissism, displayed traits of both. Rochelle needed to appear perfect to everyone and to be the center of attention at all times. While divorce is difficult for everyone, Rochelle was so fragile and empty inside, she could not recover and create a new life for herself. The insult to her self-esteem was too great. So, she relied on her daughter, behind the scenes, to prop her up. When Rochelle felt betrayed by Michelle (for example, when she had lunch with her stepmother), Rochelle lashed out with angry criticism.

And that criticism stuck around. It became part of how Michelle saw herself. Like many daughters of narcissistic mothers, Michelle grew up with a steady stream of criticism, lack of empathy, jealousy, and lack of boundaries with her mother. As an adult, she was left with an internal "gang of harsh critics" talking at her all the time, creating insecurity and self-doubt (McBride 2013).

Now let's look at how RNT might show up for you. Below is a list of common signs of RNT. Take out your journal and write down the ones that apply to you.

- I think negative, upsetting thoughts over and over, no matter how hard I try not to.

- My repetitive, negative thoughts impact how I feel about myself, my relationships, or other situations, such as work or school.

- My repetitive, negative thoughts impact how I behave in relationships, at work, at school, or in other everyday situations.

- I wish I could have better control over my repetitive negative thoughts.

- I would feel freer if I didn't have these repetitive negative thoughts.

Now that you have a better understanding of how you experience RNT, let's explore in more detail how RNT might impact you.

Why You Experience RNT

Like the *Where's Waldo?* character, repetitive negative thinking can show up everywhere. Perhaps you want to take a class, but the idea of walking into a room of strangers fills you with dread. *Everyone will look at me. They'll think I don't belong here.* Perhaps you never speak up at your condo's board meeting. Everyone talks at the same time. Maybe you can't stop thinking about how your boyfriend told you that he has to work late on Friday and can't go out. *Does he want to break up with you?* You couldn't sleep thinking about it. Or maybe you can't get your mind off how you got upset that your daughter didn't get invited to a birthday party and you sent an angry email to the birthday girl's mother. You apologized, but you're berating yourself, weeks later.

As the daughter of a narcissistic mother, you likely had several experiences growing up (and may continue to!) that make you vulnerable to RNT. Below are three common patterns that may sound familiar to you.

You learned to stay in your own head. This may have happened for a number of reasons. Your mother may have needed to be the center of attention at all times. If you had a grandiose mother, perhaps she talked nonstop about herself, and you, and probably others, were her audience. If you had a vulnerable mother, perhaps she required that you constantly take care of her. Either way, there was no room left for you to express your thoughts and feelings. Expressing your thoughts and feelings is a skill that takes practice, just like hitting a tennis ball or playing the piano.

You learned to judge your thoughts and feelings. If you *did* express your thoughts and feelings, your mother may have gotten angry or depressed or mocked your emotions, especially if she felt criticized. Like many people with narcissistic parents, your mother's critical voice became your own. When you're told that your thoughts and feelings are wrong, even worthy of mocking and contempt, the message to your inner self is: *There is something wrong with you.* This is not surprising and certainly not your fault. People "deeply internalize their parents' criticisms, meaning that the disparaging running commentary they hear inside their own head is often a reflection of parental voices," explains Kristin Neff (2011, 25) in her book *Self-Compassion.* The safest place to keep your thoughts and feelings was inside your own mind.

You learned to doubt your thoughts and feelings. In chapter 4, you learned about gaslighting. Remember, gaslighting is the way in which your mother made you doubt your sense of reality and your own feelings. What's the connection between a mother's gaslighting and the development of RNT in the daughter? Let's say your mother is a "denier." Remember Sarah, whose mother acted as if she never belittled Sarah about her schoolwork? That experience left Sarah stuck in her head, questioning herself, trying to figure out where she went wrong. If you were led to doubt yourself in any way, you may be stuck thinking about all the things you might get wrong in life, like Michelle.

"I think I'm a good mother," Michelle said in therapy. "But I question myself all the time, trying hard not to do what my mother would have done. I listen and support my kids' interests. I want to get everything

right. I lie awake at night worrying. Are they doing too many activities? Not enough? Should I help more with their homework? Less? Last month I said something to a friend I thought she might find insensitive. I was sure she I offended her. I feel so ashamed and guilty. I've been avoiding her even though I love to spend time with her. Now she's probably really thinking something's wrong! It's like I hear my mother's voice in my head all day long, telling me I did something wrong. And now it's my voice. I'm my own worst enemy."

Over time, Michelle gained new perspectives on her anxious mind. She practiced willingness to experience whatever she felt and thought—whatever showed upside her—knowing she could not control those internal events anyway. Instead, she could step back from these experiences, look at them in a different way, and focus on the important things in her life (Mazza 2020). Next, let's look at the skills Michelle embraced.

Determining the Difference Between Signals and Noise

As unpleasant as RNT and its cousin anxiety feel, they are necessary to our survival, and we don't want to get rid of them. Anxiety keeps us safe. But sometimes our nervous systems respond as if we are in danger when we are not. The metaphor of a smoke detector helps when it comes to understanding anxiety. Has the smoke detector in your kitchen ever gone off because the cookies burnt when you were baking? Almost everyone has had that experience. What do you do? You take the cookies out, turn off the oven, and open the windows. You don't call 911 to summon the fire department. You don't remove the smoke detectors so an incident like that never happens again.

You rely on that smoke detector, that alarm, even though it hurts your ears and makes your heart pound and your palms sweat. You need the smoke alarm, even though sometimes it gives you false alarms. That is, it tells you there is an emergency, when there's a small problem to solve. The thing is, our bodies don't know the difference between a real emergency (the house is on fire) and burnt cookies (open the windows). Our bodies do what they are programmed to do. They kick into the fight-flight-or-freeze response, which you probably heard of. Before you have a chance to think and register that you are really safe, a jolt of adrenaline and other stress-related hormones flood your body. These hormones prepare you to save yourself in vital ways. Therefore, a smoke alarm is a useful "signal."

When it comes to thoughts, there is a difference between *signal thoughts* and *noise thoughts*. Signal thoughts give you helpful information, even if they are worry-related. Signal thoughts are ones you should pay attention to because you can act on them or solve a problem.

In contrast, noise thoughts do not provide helpful information that you can use to take helpful action or solve a problem. Noise thoughts are like the static on a radio. When your car radio is stuck between stations and sounds like static, what do you do? Do you listen closely, trying to figure out the song or what someone is saying? Probably not. The static, or noise, is not helpful or entertaining. Instead, you tune to a station that comes in clearly and pay attention to that. Here's how learning about the difference between signal and noise thoughts helped Michelle with RNT.

> Michelle learned she couldn't turn off worry thoughts, just like she couldn't get rid of that "smoke alarm" in her brain or never have "static" on her radio again. At her next appointment, Michelle reported: "Last week I started having those thoughts about Alex's bar mitzvah. What if he gets sick? What if my mother causes a problem? Then I reminded myself that these are 'noise' thoughts and I can't do anything about them. I'm just focusing on what's really important. This is such an important day for Alex, and all our friends and family will be there. Not just my mother. The worries are still there, but I know they are just noise. I also was worried that the music would be too loud. That was a signal thought. So I spoke to the DJ, and he's going to keep it down. Music is important, but it's also important that people be able to talk with each other. I'm more relaxed and can pay attention to Alex. That's what counts!"

Now it's your turn to identify the different types of thoughts. In your journal, respond to the following questions:

- What are some of your "noise" thoughts?

- What are some of your "signal" thoughts?

- Think back to the values you identified in chapter 2. How does connecting with what matters to you help when noise or signal thoughts show up?

- What actions can you take, guided by your values, when these thoughts show up?

Externalizing Your Anxiety

When you externalize your anxiety, you think of your RNT as something outside yourself. You give your RNT a name, as if it's a character with its own identify. This makes your RNT something separate from you. You can "talk" to your RNT, creating a new "relationship" with your anxiety. Some daughters call their RNT their "worry voice." Some women name it after a character in a book, movie, or TV show. Another daughter called her inner self-doubting, shaming voice "Regina," after the infamous Queen Bee in the *Mean Girls* movie. It's important to remember that you're not trying to change or control your thoughts. You're not trying to stop them or shove them down. That is a losing battle there is no need to fight. Let's look at Lauren's story, and how this skill helped her.

> *Lauren is twenty-nine years old and about to graduate with her master's degree in elementary education. Lauren always wanted to teach young children. However, to Lauren's mother, Adele, a prominent scientist, "wiping runny noses" is not an acceptable career for her daughter.*
>
> *Lauren spent her years after college as a research assistant in a scientific lab, convincing herself that she too should be a scientist. She beat herself up for hating her job, which she should have been grateful for. No matter how hard she tried, Lauren could not help feeling flawed and unworthy. Lauren named her worry voice "Aunt Marge" after Harry Potter's nasty relative. Here are strategies that Lauren used to deal with "Aunt Marge" and that you can use too.*
>
> **Make friends with her**. *"Hey, Aunt Marge. Thanks, for showing up in class today. Take one of these little seats. I'm sure the kids will be happy to see you."*

Lower her voice. *Lauren imagined turning down the volume on Aunt Marge's voice. She could hear her whispering in the background, but since she barely heard her, it didn't matter. Soon she forgot she was there.*

Give her a silly voice. *Lauren repeated Aunt Marge's words out loud in a funny voice. The best was when she made her a California valley girl. Aunt Marge's shaming comments lost all their punch when she sounded like she popped out of a teen movie.*

Ignore her. *Lauren learned that her RNT felt like a bully in her mind. And as with any bully, sometimes it needed to be ignored. It was a relief to Lauren to know that she didn't have to stop or control the bully. She could just go about her day, doing what mattered to her, and not pay so much attention to her.*

In your journal, write about your RNT character. If you prefer, you can draw it. Then think about a situation that has been causing you RNT lately. For this exercise, it's best to choose a situation that is causing you a medium amount of distress, maybe a 3 or 4 on a scale of 0 to 10. Consider each of the following strategies and write how you would respond to your character.

- Make friends with her.

- Lower her voice.

- Give her a silly voice.

- Ignore her.

Identifying the Five Ways Your Mind Bullies You

There are five common unhelpful thinking patterns. The goal is not to change your thoughts. However, just like it helps to name your worry like a character, it helps to label the different types of worry thoughts that make up RNT. Let's take a look at Peggy's story and how it helped her identify and label different parts of her RNT.

> Peggy, age sixty, travels from Maine several times a year to see her elderly mother, Mildred, at her assisted living home in Georgia. "I dread these trips for weeks," Peggy explains. "I could move my mother to live near me, but I don't want to. She still cuts me down like I'm a fourteen-year-old who didn't do her homework. Last time, when I arrived, she commented on how wrinkled my clothes were. I just got off the plane! I know I shouldn't let her get to me, but I feel angry, which makes me feel worse, like I'm so petty. When I get home, I think about what she said to me. That's all I think about, even when I'm going for a run, when I usually forget about everything. She's the one stuck in a nursing home. Why can't I be nicer?"

Here are how the five common thinking patterns play out for Peggy.

Black-and-white thinking is when you see things in extremes. Things are either-or, with no shades of gray. When Peggy thought: *If I don't move my mother to live near me, I'm a terrible daughter,* she labeled that thought "black-and-white thinking."

Minimizing or maximizing is when you minimize your accomplishments and maximize your errors or flaws. When Peggy thought: *I should look forward to seeing my mother. I'm a horrible daughter,* Peggy learned to label that thought "minimizing."

Emotional reasoning is when you believe your feelings equal reality. When Peggy thought: *I feel like a crappy daughter. I must be a bad person,* she learned to label that "emotional reasoning."

Shoulds and oughts is when you give more weight to what other people expect of you and what you think they expect of you than what you think is right for you. When Peggy thought: *I should go where my husband wants on vacation instead of saying where I want to go,* she learned to label that thought "shoulds."

Catastrophizing is when you predict something terrible will happen in the future and don't consider other scenarios. When Peggy thought: *If I don't babysit my grandchild every weekend, I'll have a terrible relationship with my daughter-in-law,* she learned to label it "catastrophizing."

As Peggy practiced identifying and labeling her thoughts, she developed distance from them. She could tell which were signal thoughts and which were noise thoughts. In your journal, write examples of your thoughts in each of these categories. You can also go to http://www.newharbinger.com/50096 to download the worksheet: Understanding My Thoughts.

- Black-and-white thinking
- Minimizing or maximizing
- Emotional reasoning
- Shoulds and oughts
- Catastrophizing

Then consider how they impact you. Would it make a difference to notice and label these thoughts instead of taking them to heart or judging yourself for having them?

What do these strategies have in common? The thoughts and feelings you have in the present are related to your experiences growing up, but you don't have to be stuck with how they impact you. All of these strategies increase your level of mindfulness and self-awareness. You mindfully notice your thoughts without judging them and take actions that help you create the life you want to live. This is important because recent research has demonstrated that mindful people worry less when they focus on two parts of their mindfulness practice: nonjudging and acting with awareness (Evans and Segerstrom 2011).

In this chapter, you learned how daughters of narcissistic mothers struggle with chronic worried thoughts about the past, present, and future, a process known as repetitive negative thinking, or RNT. Daughters are vulnerable to developing RNT because growing up, they learn to stay in their heads and judge and doubt their thoughts and feelings. Those are good strategies in the short run when growing up with a mother who takes up all the space in the family. However, after reading this chapter, hopefully you learned that you have the power to become aware of and have a different relationship with your self-doubting, self-critical thoughts.

Chapter 6

Release Your Shame and Grief

As the daughter of a narcissistic mother, you probably know the "something is wrong with you" feeling very well, even if you never put words to it. It knocks you off your feet out of nowhere, like the invisible undertow in the ocean. Maybe it follows you around like a silent you-shaped shadow. Perhaps you know just when to expect it. It's predictable, but unwanted, like spring allergies or rush hour traffic. Let's look at some examples of shame.

You keep dating the same kind of people, the kind who are no good for you. Your friends are tired of hearing about how your dates stand you up or have someone else on the side and how you still give them one more chance. You're good at making excuses for these people or blaming yourself. Maybe you come on too strong and scare them off. Maybe you weren't clear that you want a relationship. Your friends say you need to pick better and watch out for red flags. But you know the truth. There's something wrong with you.

Maybe you keep saying you need to lose the same ten pounds, over and over. You exercise every day and eat healthy, but the scale creeps back up. At your yearly physical, your doctor noted she'll keep an eye on your cholesterol. You feel like a failure. What's wrong with you? Why can't you keep yourself healthy? There's no excuse.

Perhaps you logged onto Instagram, just for a minute. You've told yourself many times to stay off this app. It's emotional poison. But you can't resist. And there it is: a story of college friends out for dinner, without you. You weren't even that close to them, but still, you feel worthless. A week later, you still feel that way, convinced you must be so unimportant that you were excluded from the group.

Maybe last night you drank too much. Again. You promised yourself you wouldn't do it when your friends invited you to happy hour. It never winds up happy for you. The next morning you're hungover, late for work, and ashamed. Your next-door neighbor invited you to her recovery group. But what if you see someone you know? You vowed you'd never be like your mother. And here you are.

Perhaps you can't believe your boss hit on you again. Why do you let him get away with it? Touching your ass and his hand "accidentally" sliding across your breast. He announces layoffs are in the future. What can you do? Who would believe you? Everyone loves him.

These are all moments of shame: "that intensely painful feeling or experience of believing we are flawed and therefore unworthy of acceptance and belonging," as defined by Brené Brown (2007, 5). It's important to clarify the difference between two often-confused emotions: *shame* and *guilt*. You feel *guilt* when you've done something you feel is wrong, something that violates your sense of ethics or the kind of person you want to be. Perhaps you snapped at your partner after your coworker criticized your presentation. This violates your value of treating your partner kindly: feeling guilty *about your actions* is justified. If you didn't, your relationship might be in trouble. Your feelings of guilt can motivate you to take corrective action, apologize to your partner, and figure out what to do next time you are stressed out from work.

What if you felt shame after snapping at your partner instead of guilt? Shame is the feeling that something is deeply wrong with *you*, instead of your actions. If you feel shame, you might do or feel any of the following:

- Feel overly bad or self-critical about your behavior or that you're a terrible person

- Deny your behavior

- Get angry at your partner

- Ignore the problem

- Feel emotionally frozen and not know what to do

- Become depressed

- Become anxious

Shame shows up in disguise. It shows up in behaviors that, on the surface, seem unconnected to the matter at hand. Let's look more deeply at some areas in which shame might show up for you.

No Room for Error

You may struggle with needing to be perfect in parts of your life. When you make a mistake, do you make too big a deal of it? Perhaps you blow it out of proportion. When something doesn't go right, do you feel overly upset or angry at yourself or others?

That might be perfectionism rearing its ugly, painful head. It's not surprising that you feel that way. Shame and perfectionism go hand in hand. In your family, there was likely little room for making mistakes and learning from them. Instead, mistakes were met with criticism, not acknowledgment of your feelings and offers of ways to solve problems. Instead, your mistakes mattered in terms of how they made your mother feel: embarrassed, depressed, or angry, leaving you with the sense that "if one makes a mistake, one is a mistake" (Donaldson-Pressman and Pressman 1994, 102).

In addition, perhaps your mother was unable to tolerate her mistakes or imperfections. Remember that you learned from how you were treated growing up and from what you observed in your family. If your mother had a grandiose narcissistic style, she may have lashed out at and blamed others when she felt criticized or her errors came to light. If your mother had a vulnerable style of narcissism, she may have become depressed and withdrawn in the face of her own real or perceived flaws. Either way, your mother didn't have the emotional strength and maturity to know that no one is perfect.

Remember Sarah from chapter 4? When her mother, Roberta, was notified by the math teacher that Sarah was struggling, Roberta exploded, leaving Sarah with the feeling that not being perfect led to her mother's anger at her, and shame began to brew.

No one wants to feel shame. You'll do everything you can to avoid feeling it. That's why your mind has developed other things for you to do when it shows up. The problem is that shame is there anyway, and the things we do to avoid feeling it don't help us lead the kind of lives we want. In the next section you'll learn how to cope with shame.

Shifting Out of Shame

What are the solutions? First is making room for shame, or any painful emotion. Sometimes that process is called *acceptance*. Sometimes it's called *willingness*, meaning "being open to whatever shows up…being willing to have what is already there" (Boone, Gregg, and Coyne 2020, 55). It means being open to thoughts, physical sensations, and urges. Imagine it this way: being willing to have anything that you experience inside you, inside your skin. If the idea of "willingness" is confusing, you can imagine giving yourself *permission* to experience whatever comes up inside you. It doesn't mean you like or want any of it. It means that you're permitting yourself to have it.

In your journal, please respond to the following questions. As you write your responses, can you practice permitting yourself to have, without judgment, whatever arises within you? If you have judging thoughts, that's okay (you probably will). Just permit yourself to have those too.

- Do you struggle with needing to be perfect?

- If so, in what areas does perfectionism show up for you?

- Given what you have learned about the connection between shame, perfectionism, and being the daughter of a narcissistic mother, what have your learned about your experience of perfectionism?

Write briefly about a time you felt the need to be perfect (just a sentence or two is fine). Next time that happens:

- What will you say to yourself that's different?

- What actions will you take that are different?

- Is there a time in the past when this situation occurred and you handled it in a way that you feel good about, even a little bit?

- How did you that?

- What does it say about your strengths or character that you were able to do that?

Now that you've learned about shame and perfectionism, let's look at why shame is one of the most difficult emotions to understand and manage

The Sticking Power of Shame

Shame has been described as one of the most difficult emotions to bear. It has been called the "sleeper emotion" because it is so hard to recognize (Ashley 2020, xiii). Unfortunately, the relationship between the narcissistic mother and her daughter sets the stage for daughters to experience shame. Few mothers set out to create shame in their daughters. Most likely, *their* behavior stems from their own challenging, even traumatic, childhoods, from their own unmet needs. Nonetheless, it's important to understand why a daughter feels shame in the present so the cycle can be broken. And it can. Daughters of narcissistic mothers often have some, or all, of the following experiences.

- The mother behaved as if she were jealous of the daughter.

- The mother behaved as if she were competing with the daughter.

- The mother ignored the daughter's challenging emotions.

- The mother got angry with, belittled, or made fun of the daughter's emotions.

- The mother did not take appropriate care of the daughter's physical needs.

- The mother behaved in ways that were inappropriate or insensitive to the daughter's needs.

- The mother needed to be center of attention, either in a grandiose or vulnerable way.

What are the threads among these behaviors in terms of their impact on you? You grew up in a home in which you felt less than, small, and invisible. You learned that sometimes it was *helpful* to make yourself feel and act that way. It was a survival strategy. The problem is that the more you act that way, the more you feel small and invisible, and the worse you feel about yourself.

You learn that not only do your feelings and needs not count, but they are problems, burdens. Eventually, that sense of being invisible, with your feelings as burdens to others, becomes the "preset," sort of like the preset stations on the car radio. Those stations might not always be turned on. But it's much easier to turn them on because they're set. They're ready to go. Here's how Allison developed a sense of shame growing up.

> *Allison is forty-five years old. She's married to Justin, also forty-five, and they have two teenage sons. Allison is a magazine writer. After the birth of their second son, Justin was successfully treated for cancer. Allison feels grateful for her husband's health, their financial security, and their sons' well-being. Still, Allison feels that she doesn't deserve her good fortune. Although she contributes regularly to well-known publications, Allison lies awake every night before her byline appears, her jaw locked. Recently, she won an award for an investigative piece on chemical waste in local rivers.*
>
> *Allison went to the awards ceremony and accepted her plaque. As she was leaving, she overheard someone say: "Is she a scientist?"*
>
> *Allison flooded with shame and regret. Her face flushed; her legs wobbled. She thought:* What do you know about toxic waste? Somebody else could have done a much better job. *On the ride home, Allison's head swirled with doubts:* When she will be found out? When will "they" discover that she doesn't know what she's doing?
>
> *The next day, Justin told Allison he wants to take her and two of her closest friends out to dinner to celebrate her award. He is surprised to learn that Allison hasn't told her friends about it. "It's awkward,"* Allison admits. *"I don't want them to think I'm bragging."*

What led to that moment? Allison grew up with her father, Walter, a firefighter; her mother, Pamela, a homemaker; and her older brother, Brian. Allison was proud of her father. She remembered glowing with happiness when her class came to the fire department on class trips. She felt like a celebrity. But at home, it was a different kind of story. Allison saw that it was difficult for her mother when her father had twenty-four-hour shifts, requiring Pamela to take care of the children as well as her elderly parents who lived down the street. Pamela had high standards for herself and her children. Pamela rarely met her own expectations, and neither did Allison. Pamela was easily overwhelmed and when overwhelmed, sputtered cutting comments directed toward Allison.

Unlike her brother, who excelled in sports, Allison loved school. She spent as much time as she could in her room writing in her journals. Pamela seemed to find her bookish daughter embarrassing. Before dinner, Pamela would open Allison's door and ask sarcastically: "Are you writing in your secret diaries again?" When Allison brought home a report cards with all As and one A-, Pamela said, "If you're so smart, how come you got an A-?"

As she grew older, Allison shouldered more responsibilities. She helped her mother take care of her grandparents—running errands, cleaning, and eventually driving them to appointments. Pamela never thanked her and said, "Being a smarty-pants is not the only thing that counts in this family." Walter came home from his long shifts at the firehouse and slept. On his days off, he went to her brother's games.

In sixth grade, Pamela was driving Allison to the dentist. Allison confided to Pamela that she planned to be a famous writer when she grew up.

"Really?" Pamela replied. "What do you know about being a writer?"

Allison couldn't enjoy her success as a writer because shame worked so well. Growing up, Allison felt a deep sense of "badness" about being herself, even if she could not have put that feeling into words. Allison's strengths and interests—academics and writing—made her mother feel bad about herself, which created the cycle of cutting down Allison. Although Allison pursued a successful career, her mother's shaming words clung to her like a shadow.

How does this happen? Why do shame-inducing experiences stick around, long after they have passed, causing you to feel bad about yourself and behave in ways that you don't like or are not in your best interest? In order to understand why this happens, it's important to understand how early painful events get stored in your brain's memory bank.

Let's go back to Allison. Her mother made sarcastic, mean-spirited remarks about her that impacted Allison's sense of self-worth as a teen. Allison distracted herself and offered to help her mother. She didn't consciously think, *That felt terrible. My mother hurt my feelings. But I know it's not my fault that she talks to me this way.*

Instead, the brain gets to work dealing with this traumatic experience. Here's what happens. Say a teenage you had a painful experience with your mother. The "emotional" part of your brain, known as the limbic system, kicks into action. It releases stress chemicals or hormones, such as adrenaline and cortisol, into your bloodstream. Your muscles tighten, your heart pounds, and your stomach feels queasy. The "thinking" part of your brain, in the face of this stressful event, turns off. It gets "hijacked" by the power of the moment. In the briefest of instants, the memory of this event gets "stamped" in your emotional brain. This part of the brain stores your emotional memories. Emotional memories don't have words attached to them; they don't have a grown-up story to explain them. When your memories are stored in your brain in this way, there simply isn't time for them to "travel" to the "thinking" part of our brains, where memories get embedded with logic and language (Armstrong 2015).

Years after a painful or traumatic incident, that memory is still stored in your emotional brain. When Allison overheard someone say: "Is she a scientist?" it instantly brought back the memory of her mother's critical comments. Her body reacted as if she were fourteen years old, back in her teenage bedroom. Of course, Allison didn't even know if the person's comment was critical. Perhaps the person was amazed that a nonscientist wrote such an excellent article on toxic waste!

Here's the thing: "your emotional brain confuses similar and same" (Armstrong 2015, 10). That's what happened to Allison. Her brain couldn't tell the difference between the hurtful experiences with her mother and how they made her feel, and what was happening in the here and now.

In addition, like all emotions, shame served a purpose. It helped her "hide" and "cover up" what she really needed: to feel that she was valuable for who she was (Armstrong 2015). Next, let's how see Allison learned to uncover the pain of shame and how you can too.

Allison learned a five-part process to identify and manage the emotion of shame. In the next section, use your journal to write down your responses when indicated. Please note that these five steps can be applied to other painful emotions as well.

1. Name Shame

Write about a time when you felt not good about yourself. Please pick an incident that feels mild to moderate for you, not one that is extremely shameful. As you recall this memory, write what you notice about:

- the physical sensations in your body

- the thoughts that come into your mind

- your emotions

- the need that the feeling of shame was trying to cover up or keep you protected from.

Allison wrote about a time when she got her sons' back-to-school nights mixed up and went to the wrong school. She drove to the correct one and walked in late, only missing fifteen minutes of the presentation. Nonetheless, Allison felt horrible, as if she had failed her son in some terrible way. As Allison wrote about this memory, she noticed her jaw lock up and a sinking feeling in the pit of her stomach. She knew her reaction was excessive, but she couldn't shake it. As she learned about shame, she connected that harsh voice in her head with her experiences growing up. Remember how Pamela mocked Allison for getting an A- instead of an A?

Allison realized how Pamela was hard on herself too. Pamela expected herself to be perfect and became angry and frustrated when she wasn't. One part of Allison's "shame voice" meant she needed to be perfect. Just like if she wasn't a scientist, how could she justify earning an award for her science writing? She could never be good enough. It took Allison a lot of practice, but over time, as she experienced shame, she learned to "name" it and use the next steps to put it in perspective.

2. Name What You Value

Shame steals your sense of who you are and what is important to you. When those feelings of worthlessness are triggered, you may avoid people, places, events, or activities that are meaningful to you. Remember, this avoidance strategy helped and protected you earlier in life. However, it does not serve you well now. It's important to once again identify what's important to you.

Think about the memory you identified in part 1 above. What does it say about what is important to you in terms of leading a rich and meaningful life? For a reminder about types of values, please go to chapter 2 or look in your journal. What actions can you take to live out those values, even if it feels uncomfortable?

Allison identified that two of her core values were connecting with others and caring for the environment. When she froze in shame, she identified actions she could take so those values would impact her life. That meant Allison told her friends about her writing award even though it made her feel uncomfortable. They went out together and celebrated, just as Allison had celebrated her friends' good news in the past. This brought to life Allison's value of feeling connected to others. Allison took on more challenging writing assignments about environmental issues because caring for the environment mattered to her, and this was how she made a difference. Her mother's voice still rang in her ear ("What do you know about writing?"). However, Allison learned to step back from it and do what mattered to her.

3. Look at Shame in a Different Way

Earlier in this chapter, you learned about how shame-related events get stored away as memories in the emotional part of your brain. The memories get locked in quickly, before the logical part of your brain gets a chance to understand them. You might not have been old enough for your brain to look at those incidents and understand that a painful event was not your fault. The following questions, based on the work of trauma expert Courtney Armstrong (2015), are designed to help you step back from difficult life events and understand them from a healthier perspective.

1. Write briefly about a difficult life event. Just a few sentences are fine.

2. How did this event change how you think or feel about yourself? Other people? Life, the world, and your future?

3. What do you want to believe about the people involved in the event now? How do you want to feel around them?

4. Where are you stuck in that emotional memory?

5. How would you like to feel about yourself now?

6. What strengths, talents, or insights have you been able to develop in spite of this event?

7. What would you like to tell your younger self, from this different place you are now?

8. What would you like to believe about life, the world, and your future? Is there a way you can imagine using this experience to live your life with a greater sense of purpose, strength, or meaning?

Remember Lauren from chapter 5? Lauren worked as a lab assistant instead of becoming a kindergarten teacher to avoid feeling the painful feelings of being less than. Lauren knew that her career choice was deeply disappointing to her mother, leaving Lauren feeling that she, herself, was a deep disappointment. Here is how Lauren responded to this exercise.

1. *When I was in college, I told my mother I wanted to become a kindergarten teacher. She looked at me with such contempt. She said in her most cutting voice: "People in our family don't spend their lives wiping runny noses."*

2. *It made me feel like my dream was an embarrassment to her, like I was an embarrassment. It made me feel worthless. It made me feel that that other people would never understand me, just like my mother didn't understand me, that I would always be seen as someone wasting her talent and dishonoring her family. It made me feel hopeless, like I could never achieve my goal or really be the person I wanted to be.*

3. *I would like to understand that how my mother acted and what she said to me were about her, not me or my goals. She sees the world in a certain way, and there's nothing I can do about it.*

4. *Hearing the tone of my mother's voice. It was so contemptuous. It was the tone that upset me so much, even more than the words.*

5. *I'm a separate person from my mother. Her words might hurt me sometimes, but they are not me.*

6. *I can keep changing and growing as a person. I'm stronger than I thought. I can understand other people's feelings.*

7. *That I would go on to become a teacher, and I would be good at it. I would find my voice and find the strength to make my own choices. I would be happy working in a school. I'll have lots of friends there too.*

8. *Not everybody looks at the world the way my mother does. I can find people to connect with who share my values and appreciate me for who I am. There's more than one way to live and contribute to the world.*

The following section addresses grief and mourning because for many daughters of narcissistic mothers, the questions of shame, grief, and mourning are intertwined in complex ways.

Grief and Mourning

Even if your mother is still alive, you may feel angry and sad that you never had a "real" mother. You can't imagine what that would feel like. You wish you could get rid of these feelings. They feel like a ten-ton weight on your back.

You try to pretend you have a "normal" relationship with your mother, especially around the holidays. You don't want anyone to know how your mother treated you and how you feel about her. People will think that there is something wrong with you or maybe that you're crazy or damaged goods.

You imagine you'll feel relieved when your mother dies. In fact, you're looking forward to that day. Won't you finally feel free?

You even have had fantasies of killing your mother. You would never, ever do it. But these images just pop into your mind when she makes you feel small, mocked, or angry. Then you feel even worse about yourself: ashamed and flawed. What kind of person has thoughts like that?

Can you relate to these thoughts, emotions, or urges? If so, you are not alone. As the daughter of a narcissistic mother, you may struggle with confusing feelings of pain, self-blame, and even despair about your relationship with your mother and her impact on you. As you read earlier, practicing acceptance of your feelings is critical to moving forward. In addition, you may need to experience the particular emotion of grief. You may need to mourn the relationship you never had with your mother.

This is not easy. There are rituals and traditions that define grief and mourning. Catholics have wakes. Jews sit shiva. Westerners wear dark colors to signify they are in mourning, while white is the traditional color of bereavement in many Asian cultures. Such customs help people acknowledge the reality of death, remember the person who died, get support, and figure out who they are without the deceased in their lives (Wolfelt 2016).

However, you may experience a type of grief that doesn't have these types of traditions and rituals. It's called "ambiguous loss." The term "ambiguous loss" was coined by psychologist Pauline Boss (2002) and refers to the feeling associated with someone who is "perceived as physically present, but psychologically absent." Family members can be "preoccupied with the lost person, and think of little else, even years later" (Boss 2002). Ambiguous loss is psychological. It's unresolved. Whether your mother is living or not, your loss, your grief, is hidden. There's no ceremony. No condolence cards. No casseroles left on your doorstep. How do you mourn a relationship with a mother who was there, but not there?

> *June came to therapy when she was seventy-two years old because she was anxious and waking up multiple times at night, unable to fall back asleep. Her mother, Florence, died decades earlier. June lived alone, retired from her job in state government. With her pension, June lived comfortably, although without money to spare. When Florence died, she left her home, where June grew up, to June's brother because "he's married and needs it more than you do." June was crushed by her mother's decision. The fact that her mother left everything in the house to her brother as well added insult to injury.*
>
> *"I tried to rise above it," June reported. "I thought I did. I was always close to my niece and nephew, even though I never had great relationships with my brother or his wife." She paused, while tiny tears dampened her eyes. "I don't know why I'm so upset now. They're selling the house and moving to Florida. They never even asked me if I was interested in making an offer."*
>
> *In therapy, June lifted the lid on painful emotions she kept well-guarded throughout her life. "I always felt like a second-class citizen in my family. My mother only had eyes for my brother. I did the chores and got good grades, but that wasn't exciting to her. I never felt noticed or important."*
>
> *June mourned the relationship with her mother and how it impacted how she saw and felt about herself. She had no voice, twice, in the selling of the family home, just as she had no voice growing up.*

June's grief had many layers, although she was not aware of it until she finally came to therapy. June grieved a mother-daughter relationship she never had. She grieved feeling loved, seen, and cherished. She grieved feeling valuable and important, when she was growing up and when she was a single, working woman. And she finally grieved the loss of her family home and not having her feelings counted or considered, like that "second-class citizen."

Practice: Giving Voice to Grief

Let's do something a little different. Please answer the following writing prompts in your journal with your mother in mind. Responding to these statements may be challenging, so take it slow. It may help to complete this practice or share your responses with a therapist, trusted friend, or other supportive person.

- I wish:

- It's important to me that you know:

- It was very difficult for me when you:

- I don't think you realize that:

- I needed you to:

- I never told you that I:

- My fondest memory of you is:

- My most difficult memory of you is:

- Because of our relationship, I struggle with:

- Because of our relationship, I have the following strengths:

- I am so proud that I:

- I wonder if you knew that:

- My greatest accomplishments are:

- When I have grieved you enough, I will:

- The most important thing I have learned from our relationship is:

(Adapted with permission from the work of Robert Neimeyer, PhD.)

These are good questions to reread and reflect on over time. Remember that all sorts of thoughts, emotions, memories, and urges will come up, and you can allow them to be there. You can notice them, step back from them, and do things that matter to *you*. Most importantly, talk to yourself with kindness and compassion, just as you would talk to a friend who is grieving.

In this chapter you learned about the complicated emotion of shame. You learned about what it is, why you experience it, and how you can cope with it. You learned about complicated grief and how to mourn the loss of a relationship you never had. In the next chapter, you'll learn more about emotions: how you struggle with knowing what you feel and handling emotions.

Chapter 7

Soothe Your Emotional
Roller Coaster

As the daughter of a narcissist mother, the following scenarios may sound familiar to you.

When others talk about their feelings, you're baffled because you don't know what you feel most of the time. You could say you feel numb, but that's not really a feeling.

You feel your emotions, alright. If only what you felt and how you responded matched the situation. At your child's school, a poster reads: "Little problem, little reaction." You can't seem to pull that off. You thought you'd lose your mind in the traffic jam this morning. When you got to your meeting, your hands were covered in hives—your "tell" for stress. This is no way to live.

You feel the appropriate reactions for situations. Only they don't last. For example, you felt irritated when your teenager didn't do his chores *again* last night. And then you feel guilty for feeling irritated. You want to have a good relationship with him. You think: *Good mothers don't feel this. Don't all teenagers forget their chores?* So you him let him off the hook, again.

You feel like an emotional sponge, absorbing everyone else's feelings, especially their anger, sadness, and anxiety. It gets heavy being that sponge. If only you could wring yourself out. Or better yet, not absorb all those emotions in the first place. Your coworker's partner lost her job last month, and she can't stop talking about how worried she is. You feel horrible for her and can't stop thinking about how to help. Your husband says it's not your responsibility. So why does it feel that way?

Maybe your friend always cancels plans at the last minute, but you reschedule. Your spouse doesn't understand why you do that. Aren't you fed up? No, you're not; it's just okay. Or maybe you know when you feel something. But if it doesn't feel good, you squash it. There are so many ways to do it: wine, binge-watching Netflix, three exercise classes in a row, online shopping, vaping, Tinder, and of course, your phone, always at the ready. Some of these behaviors are not harmful when done in moderation. But when you use them to cover up your painful feelings over and over, it's another story.

In this chapter, you'll discover how being raised by a narcissistic mother impacted your ability to handle your own and others' emotions. First, you'll get a brief overview of how children learn about emotions so you can better understand what happened in your family. Next, you'll learn why your mother had such difficulty understanding her feelings and responding to yours with empathy.

How Children Learn to Handle Emotions

When children are growing up, they learn how to handle emotions in two primary ways: (1) in the context of their relationship with their parents or primary caregivers and (2) by observing how their parents or primary care-givers handle their own emotions.

Children show their emotions in school all day long. They cry; they are frustrated and silly. How teachers respond to those emotions leave lasting lessons. Children also learn about emotions through play and their relationships with other children. As adolescents, they learn about emotions in early romantic relationships. But people's internal "blueprints" for understanding and handling emotions are laid down through their early relationships with parents or caregivers.

Let's say you started on a healthy road when it comes to learning about emotions. Your primary caregiver was able to be your "emotion coach" (Gottman 1998). She would:

- be aware of your emotions

- see your emotions as an opportunity to get close to you and teach you

- listen to you with empathy and validate your feelings

- label your emotions with words you can understand

- help you figure out appropriate ways to solve a problem or deal with an upsetting situation.

When these interactions happen enough of the time (remember, no parent is perfect!), you develop what is known as emotional intelligence to the degree you are able based on your genetics and temperament (Goleman 1995). When you are emotionally intelligent, you:

- know what you feel

- understand how your feelings impact yourself and others

- think ahead about how your emotional reactions impact yourself and others, so you don't act impulsively

- harness your emotions to achieve your goals and persevere when things get tough

- empathize with the feelings of others

- can draw on your emotions to form healthy relationships and communicate respectfully and positively to others.

But what if you were raised by a narcissistic mother? Your mother was your earliest teacher when it came to learning about your emotions, having self-compassion for them, and developing the skills to manage them effectively. *However, your mother could not teach you skills that she simply did not have herself.* Let's look more closely at the psychological makeup of narcissistic mothers and how it impacted their daughters' capacity to be their own "emotion coach" (Gottman 1998).

When Your Mother Is Unable to Identify Her Emotions and Yours

Your mother struggled to identify her own emotions and put them into words. This, in turn, impacted her ability to manage her own emotions. This struggle contributed to her difficulty being able to know what *you* were feeling and to understand and process your emotions (Ronningstam 2017).

The mental health profession used to believe that narcissists simply had no empathy. Recent research reveals that empathy in narcissists is more like a slice of Swiss cheese: full of holes (Baskin-Sommers et al. 2014). That means your mother may have had little to no empathy for your feelings. She may have empathized sometimes. It depended on what was going on in her life or how she was feeling inside. She may have showed care and understanding for your feelings if she felt doing so reflected well on her (maybe it was a public show of empathy). The bottom line is you never knew when you would receive empathy from her. When it came to helping you through difficult situations or reveling in your joys, your mother's reactions were unpredictable. They were based on her inner world, not on what was going on in your world.

Other factors complicate how empathetic a narcissistic mother can be. Narcissists may believe they are more empathetic than they actually are. They might not *want* to be empathetic because they fear loss of control or appearing vulnerable. A laboratory study found that narcissists have negative reactions while watching others in positive experiences (Baskin-Sommers et al. 2014). In addition, research indicates that narcissists can display empathy when it helps them feel in control, feel good about themselves, or is in their best interest. It's no wonder that narcissistic mothers have such difficulty managing their emotions and being empathetic and supportive toward their daughters.

What happens when a mother has little or no idea what she's feeling and even less ability to handle her emotions in a mature way? Below are three patterns commonly seen in families with a narcissistic mother. Your family may have exhibited one of these styles or a mixture of all of them.

The Volcano Mother

If you grew up with a volcano mother, your mother erupted unpredictably in the face of feelings. You never knew what you were walking into. Remember that inside, you mother struggles with "deep-seated insecurity" and her "self-esteem is continually under threat" (Durvasula 2021, 10). Let's say as a teenager, you rolled your eyes or spoke too saucily. For the volcano mother, it's as if her sense of self is under attack. So she attacks back, yelling that she can't stand you.

What could have happened differently? A mother with a stronger sense of self could have felt hurt and angry, while recognizing that such behavior is normal, although unpleasant, with teenagers. She could have stepped back, setting a limit with you firmly and respectfully. You, in turn, would leave the interaction with your dignity and connection to your mother intact. You would experience that your mother's love does not depend on always pleasing her or being perfect.

If you were raised by a volcano mother, you may be hypervigilant: constantly on the lookout for what other people are feeling or doing. In addition, you try to fix things before a potential explosion occurs. You tend to overcorrect or leap before you look. There is part of you, which you might not even be aware of, that wants to avoid those explosions. So, you people-please, read into things, do too much—anything to keep the peace. Often, this pattern of behavior occurs at your own expense or that of your well-being.

Daughters of volcano mothers struggle with second-guessing themselves, low self-esteem, and self-blame. As a child, it's natural to think: *Maybe I caused Mom to act this way. Maybe it's my fault.*

The "Blinders-On" Mother

If you grew up with a blinders-on mother, your mother didn't see when you expressed your feelings, as if they didn't exist. If you had a grandiose mother, perhaps she was always talking about herself or was too busy with her own pursuits to notice what was happening with you. If you had a vulnerable narcissistic mother, she might have been depressed, relying on you to support and take care of her.

The blinders-on mother might ignore your feelings by putting them down, mocking, or criticizing them. She might say you're being too sensitive or overreacting. These are all ways to not see or "unsee" your feelings.

If you were raised by a blinders-on mother, you learned to shove your feelings deep down inside or even to numb them. You learned that no matter how upset or angry you were, or even joyful or proud, it would not be acknowledged. Your mother's ability to empathize with your emotions was highly impaired. When you were sad, you were speaking a language she could not understand.

It's not surprising that as an adult you don't know what you feel. As you read earlier in the chapter, children learn about their emotions when they are labeled and validated. You learned to protect your unseen and unvalidated emotions by pushing them away or telling yourself that feelings are unnecessary or wrong. That was a smart thing to do at the time because it protected you when no one noticed your feelings. But it's not so helpful now. As an adult, you hear your mother's voice in your head when it comes to your emotions.

The "It's Your Fault" Mother

If you grew up with an it's-your-fault mother, then feelings were big problems—both her feelings and yours. This pattern is related to some of the key features of narcissism: the narcissist's intense sensitivity to perceived criticism and need for admiration all rolled up in being empty and insecure inside. If your mother felt judged, left out, or criticized (feelings no one likes!), it was unbearable to her, as if her very sense of self was being threatened. She protected it by lashing out at you—it's your fault she has to work late and her boss doesn't promote her.

Similarly, let's say you cried because you weren't invited to the popular kids' party. Here's a validating response: "Wow, honey, that sounds really hard. I'm so sorry about that." However, a narcissistic mother feels rejected herself (vulnerable style) or enraged that you didn't get an invitation you were entitled to (grandiose style). She's not aware she feels this way and can't separate her feelings from your needs. Perhaps she said something like: "What did you do to not get invited?"

When you grow up with an it's-your-fault mother, you live in fear of your feelings. They signal feeling guilty and flawed. You feel responsible for everything and blame yourself for things that are not your fault. Talking to yourself in a kind and compassionate way is like a foreign language. You take on more than you can handle, trying to make up for your flaws. When you make a mistake (Who doesn't?), it may be hard to admit because your fear of retribution is so great.

This is a good time to get out your journal and respond to the following questions. Take your time. It's possible that upsetting memories or feelings will show up. If they do, what practices have you learned so far that could help you, such as mindfulness, self-compassion, or deep breathing? Then consider which of these styles most closely describes your mother: the volcano mother, the blinders-on mother, or the it's-your-fault mother.

- Can you describe a specific time that your mother responded to your emotions in one of the above styles or in a combination of the styles?

- How did that impact you at the time?

- How has her style of responding to your emotions continued to impact you?

- Have you learned anything new or surprising about the connection between your mother's emotional style and how you handle emotions?

- How does it help to understand this connection?

You just learned about why and how you struggle with emotions. Let's look at Amanda's story to see how this plays out for a daughter of a narcissistic mother.

Amanda, age twenty-two, recently graduated from college and started a prestigious training program for a financial services company. Amanda pushes herself hard. She works ten- and sometimes twelve-hour days. Then she comes home and runs for eight to ten miles, finishing up with Pilates on YouTube. Her roommate noticed that she lives on coffee and yogurt and expressed concern for Amanda's well-being. "I'm fine," Amanda told her. "I feel great."

Exhausted, Amanda collapses at night, but can't fall asleep for two hours. Her mind spins with possible mistakes she made at work. Her performance is critical in getting hired for a permanent position.

The other members of the training program seem so sure of themselves. Amanda is convinced she is the only one with so much self-doubt. They go out for lunch together, but Amanda wouldn't dream of it. She has to double- and even triple-check her work to make sure there are no mistakes in her reports. And then there's her supervisor, Alicia. Alicia is smart, beautiful, and no-nonsense and was promoted to department head by the time she was thirty. Once Alicia told their team that a joint presentation "could have been better." Amanda was sure she was looking right at her.

Amanda grew up with her parents, Patty and Chad, and her younger brother, Ryan. Both Patty and Chad were college athletes and expected Amanda and Ryan to follow in their sneakered footsteps. Amanda was athletically gifted. College basketball coaches eyed her as early as eighth grade as she played with club teams around her town, then the state, the country, and even Europe. Between homework and basketball, Amanda had little time for friends or other activities. Patty attended every practice and game, providing Amanda with blow-by-blow critiques: "Your head wasn't in the game! How are you going to start if you play like that?"

Amanda stayed silent on the drives home. She'd get back to the house, take a shower, and head to her room for homework. Once she told her mother that she'd like to try out for the school play. Patty snorted with laughter: "And miss practice? That's not how you get recruited for D-1. I gave up my career for your basketball." Before having kids, Patty was a highly paid attorney.

Some nights Amanda was so discouraged she lay on her bed and cried. She knew her mother could hear, but Patty never checked on her. She never knocked on the door and asked how Patty was doing. The next morning Patty acted as if everything was fine, rushing Amanda and her brother to the bus, basketball gear in tow. When Amanda was in tenth grade, a university made her an offer to play basketball unofficially. Patty wanted her to tell the coach she would play for this school. Amanda sobbed in her guidance counselor's office.

"I'm only fifteen! I don't know where I want to go to college!" Patty would hear none of it, and Amanda agreed to go to the school.

Then, in the spring of her senior year, disaster hit. Struck by senioritis, regimented Amanda skateboarded for the first time with a friend. Flying off a ramp, Amanda broke her leg. Hearing how long her recovery would take, the college basketball coach withdrew her spot on the team.

Patty was enraged. "After all our hard work! After everything I've done for you!" It was as if the loss was all Patty's. Patty didn't attend Amanda's high school graduation, saying she had thrown her back out.

Amanda learned that her feelings don't count. As an adult, she stuffs them down with work, perfectionism, and exercise. She sees being kind to herself, even having fun, as a weakness, and assumes responsibility for anything that goes wrong. Finally, Amanda goes to the doctor when she notices her dark curly hair in clumps swirling around the shower drain. Her doctor gently points out her eight-pound weight loss and that her last period was three months ago. Amanda accepts her doctor's referral to a therapist specializing in eating disorders. She begins the journey to see the connection between her mother's voice in her head, always pushing her to do more, the relentless inner voice of perfection, and "running from" her feelings. She begins to identify her own feelings and needs and to validate them for herself.

Looking into Patty's inner emotional world, what would we see? Like all people with narcissism, Patty relied solely on things outside herself—other people's behavior, accomplishments, compliments, material goods—to feel good about herself. We all do this to some degree. It becomes a problem when you rely on things that are out of your control to keep your mood, sense of self-worth, and self-control in check. That is the core dilemma for the narcissistic mother.

In Patty's family, what mattered was how things looked on the outside. Although her mother had numerous affairs that Patty and her sister knew about, the family was expert at pretending everything was fine. Patty's stay-at-home mother ran the PTO, Walk for Hunger, and Race for a Cure. Patty mastered smiling her way through events as people acclaimed her mother's contributions. Patty's mother never told her she was proud of her, although other people did: "Your mother is so thrilled that you got into law school." Patty was baffled. Her mother never told her that.

Patty learned to feel safe by keeping up façades. She did so, playing college sports and succeeding in law. Then she became a mother, and her children took on the job of helping Patty keep up appearances and protecting her from inner pain. Only she couldn't control what happened with her daughter, Amanda, the same way she could with her own athletics and academics. Nor did Patty have any model for understanding and validating a daughter's emotions.

Patty couldn't see Amanda as separate from herself, with her own needs, desires, and feelings. When Amanda wanted to try out for the play or hold off on committing to a college, it threatened Patty's sense of security in the world.

Generally, when it comes to handling our emotions, it helps to pause and reflect, even for a moment. Of course, when we're in a life-threatening emergency, our brains tell us to react immediately to get out of danger. If you're crossing the street and see a car speeding your way, you should jump back on the curb. Pronto. However, in most situations, it helps to pause and respond, not react without thinking first. When you were raised by a narcissistic mother, you might not have developed a set of fully equipped skills to label your emotions, accept and validate them, and handle them with care for yourself and others. Next is a practice to help you identify, validate, and manage your feelings more effectively. SLOW helps you do that.

Practice: SLOW

SLOW is a flexible four-step process to identify your feelings and choose how to handle them with compassion. You can use it anytime, anywhere. Even if you can't remember the four steps, you only have to remember the word SLOW. It works in any situation where an emotion comes up, especially a strong, challenging emotion.

S: Slow Down

Pause. Give your body and mind time to settle down. Here are several things you can do to slow down. With some of them, no one even has to know that you are doing them.

- Take slow, deep breaths. Try to make your out-breath longer than your in-breath to activate the relaxation response.

- Press your feet firmly into the floor. Press your hands firmly together, against your thighs, or against the wall.

- Look around. Name three things you can see, hear, smell, touch, or taste.

- Move your body. Walk, stretch, jump, or flex your feet and hands.

L: Look Inside and Identify

What are you feeling? You have to know what you're feeling to determine what to do about it. You're working on expanding your emotional dictionary.

Primary emotions. Ask yourself if you feel one of the six primary emotions identified by psychologist Paul Ekman (1999):

- sadness

- happiness

- fear

- anger

- surprise

- disgust

Of course, there are many more words for emotions! In building your emotional dictionary, you're learning nuanced words for your six primary emotions. The more words you know, the more you can accurately pinpoint your feelings. Take the emotion of fear. At the mildest end, you may feel "nervous." In the middle, you might feel "alarmed." At the far end of the spectrum, you feel "petrified." How do those emotions feel different? Next, be on the lookout for your secondary emotion(s).

Secondary emotions. Secondary emotions occur in response to primary emotions (Van Dijk 2012). They are how you judge or interpret your feelings. You do this based on what you learned about feelings when you were growing up. Often, your secondary emotion undermines your primary emotion.

Think back to an example from the opening of the chapter. You feel a flash of anger when your friend cancelled your plans, again, at the last minute. Whenever you showed anger growing up, perhaps your mother said, "You're so sensitive." Maybe she engaged in gaslighting behavior and told you that what you're angry about never really happened. In the present, you will feel guilt when anger shows up; the guilt is your secondary emotion. As an adult, your automatic reaction, which may be *out of your awareness*, is to tell yourself you don't feel angry and to justify your friend's behavior.

O: Open Up by Accepting and Validating Your Emotions

To accept means to *allow* yourself to have the feeling, even if is uncomfortable. It doesn't mean you like it or want it. The harder we try to push a feeling away, the more it pops up, like an old-fashioned jack-in-the-box toy. Acceptance is not easy and takes practice our whole lives. However, not accepting our feelings is like not accepting the weather. We have no control over the weather, even if it rains on our whole vacation at the beach! What we can do is acknowledge and accept how frustrated we feel and validate it.

To validate means acknowledging our feelings with kindness and compassion. Most daughters of narcissistic mothers are much better at doing this for others than for themselves. Your self-talk might sound like: "It's really hard to have it rain this whole week. It's so disappointing." If your secondary emotion of guilt kicks in, you might be tempted to invalidate yourself and say: "Don't be a baby. Things can't always go your way. That's life." The problem is that this makes us feel worse and can make us feel more frustrated and irritable. It can make it harder for us to treat ourselves, and then others, with compassion. So it helps to open up to what you are feeling. You can do that by waiting.

W: Wait and Choose a Response with Compassion

Now that you have slowed down, and identified, accepted, and validated your emotions to the best of your ability, you can thoughtfully choose (instead of impulsively jumping on) your next step. That may be something other people can't see (how you're thinking about a situation) or something other people can see (what you say or do). There are many options here, and you'll learn more strategies in the chapter on boundaries and healthy communication (chapter 9). Here are some ideas.

Internal responses: See above (slow down, accept, validate).

External responses: Set a limit, speak up, take a chance, do something a different way, take a break.

How can you best practice SLOW in your life? Practice one step at a time. It helps to write the steps on your phone or on an index card for a reminder. This week, choose one step or steps to practice. In your journal, record what happens when you practice slowing down or waiting before you respond when you have a strong emotion.

- What happens when you do this?
- How does it make a difference for you? For others?
- Did you notice anything different in how your body felt?
- What does it say about you—your strengths, resources, characteristics—that you were able to do that?

In this chapter, you learned about emotions: how they work, why you struggle with them, and how you can learn to identify and handle them in new ways. This knowledge will serve you well as you identify your core strengths and building confidence in the next chapter.

Chapter 8

Find Your Core Strengths and Build Confidence

As the daughter of a narcissistic mother, chances are you're lacking confidence in a certain area of your life. Perhaps you don't "own" or are even not aware of your strengths and unique abilities. Often women with a narcissistic parent have an inner critic or a voice of doubt that shows up in some important area of life. You may be tired of hearing the voice of self-doubt. It tells you to stay small and invisible and never to ask for help. It can be hard to tell if it's your voice or your mother's. In this chapter, we'll take a deep dive into why you doubt yourself and undercut your own dreams and best interests. We'll explore the steps you can take to change those patterns.

Do any of the following statements sound familiar to you? As the daughter of a narcissistic mother, you might say these things to yourself every day. Or perhaps these beliefs lurk silently inside your mind. Either way, they impact how you feel, think, and act, even if you are not aware that they do.

"I don't matter."

"Who am I to...?"

"How dare I...?"

"I don't deserve..."

"I cause trouble when I..."

"I never should have…"

"Next time, I won't…"

"_____ is more important than me."

"How could I have felt that way?"

"I never should have asked for…"

"I could never…"

Clarifying Confidence

What is confidence anyway? Like narcissism, the concept of confidence has a complicated history. Let's start by throwing out the idea that confidence is something you "have," like good eye-hand coordination or an eye for design. Rather, confidence is something you build. Unfortunately, we live in a culture of social media self-promotion, which makes it seem like everyone and her sister is a rock star (or feels like one). First, authentic confidence is the belief that you can *master* skills or challenges that you take on.

Mastery means that when you hit a problem, you look at it in a different way and you keep going. You know you might, or might not, overcome the challenges. But you feel good enough about yourself and can cheerlead yourself enough to try anyway. As journalists Katty Kay and Claire Shipman (2014) write in *The Confidence Code: The Science and Art of Self-Assurance—What Women Should Know*: "Confidence is the stuff that turns thoughts into action" (50).

Sometimes you decide that a challenge is not for you, and that's okay too. You can acknowledge your decision, with compassion and kindness for yourself, and move on. Second, confidence is something more elusive. It's a sense you have about yourself. It's a feeling of self-assurance. It's that feeling of being "enough."

The Building Blocks of Confidence

According to Madeline Levine (2012), author of *Teach Your Children Well: Parenting for Authentic Success*, parents who instill the building blocks of confidence in their children strive to do the following:

- Encourage their children to solve problems independently

- Seek help when they can't solve problems independently

- Teach their children to self-soothe

- Teach their children that there is more than one way to solve a problem

- Support their children with enthusiasm and empathy

- Allow their children to take care of themselves in age-appropriate ways

- Teach their children self-control

- Teach their children that they can make a difference in their own lives

- Love their children for who they are, not who they want them to be

The foundation of confidence is laid, little by little, when children feel that their parents expect them to try new things, fail, and pick themselves up again and keep going, grounded with love, support, and acceptance. Just as importantly, parents don't fall apart in the face of their child's struggles. Perhaps you can see from this list the challenges a mother with narcissistic traits faces in helping her daughter build confidence because she herself lacks the required skills, such as emotional self-control and flexibility.

How Your Seeds of Self-Doubt Got Planted

Now that you know what confidence is and how it is developed, let's review your experiences growing up and see how they connect with your struggles with confidence. *Note: Please bear in mind that many other factors in our society influence the development of confidence, the belief that one can overcome difficulties in life. These factors include sexism, institutional racism, poverty, discrimination against the LGBTQ+ community, cultural norms, ableism, and individual differences, such as learning disabilities. As you read and review your own experience, please keep in mind how all these concerns may play into your confidence story.*

Below is a list of experiences that may sound familiar to you and that may have impacted your sense of confidence as you were growing up.

- Your mother expected too much of you or not enough.

- Your mother did not support your interests or was unreliable in supporting your interests.

- Your mother expected you to do things that were inappropriate for your age or ability.

- Your mother supported your interests if they aligned with her interests.

- Your mother pressured you to engage in interests or activities that you did not want to.

- Your mother rarely or never praised your successes.

- Your mother praised or noticed your successes *only*, not your effort or trying.

- Your mother took credit for your successes.

- Your mother seemed jealous or envious of your successes.

- Your mother mocked or showed contempt for your efforts, successes, or failures.

- Your mother displayed inappropriate boundaries when it came to your interests.

- Your mother was dishonest or cheated when it came to your interests or ones she supported.

Let's see how the issue of confidence shows up in Lisa, the daughter of a narcissistic mother.

Lisa, age thirty-five, stays home to raise her two children. The worst part of her day? Waiting at the bus stop with the other moms and dads. Sometimes parenting seems like a competitive sport, with the other parents casually mentioning whose first grader reads Harry Potter or whose two-year-old "potty-trained herself in one day!" It feels like Lisa has read every parenting book on the market. She follows endless "mommy blogs." She loves being a mother. The problem is her anxiety. She's always second-guessing herself and her decisions about the children. Her husband, Arjun, doesn't get it.

"You're such a great mother," he reassures Lisa, as she worries about not practicing the kind of parenting in which your child sleeps in the same bed with you, like her friend Meredith does. She worries that she stays home. She worries about going back to work. Lisa knows some of this worrying is normal for mothers and that she's privileged to have a choice, but for her, it feels so painful, like a knife of self-doubt piercing her peace with her family.

Lisa grew up with her parents and older brother in a comfortable Miami suburb. Both her parents were highly paid professionals. In their free time, her parents golfed and played tennis at the country club. Lisa and her brother, Lucas, spent their free time hanging around at home or at the club, sometimes doing nothing, sometimes drinking a lot. This was easy since their parents weren't paying attention. In ninth grade, one of Lisa's teachers pointed out that since she was so good at French, it would be great if she could stay after school and participate in the tutoring program. However, Lisa's mother said she couldn't pick her up because of her tennis game. Lisa kept her grades up and won a French award at graduation. At graduation, Lisa's mother elbowed her way through the crowd, grabbed the head of the French department, and hugged him. "I knew she would win that award. That's because we went to Saint Martin every winter so she could speak French," she announced.

Growing up, Lisa lived a well-cared-for life. All her basic needs were met and then some. What Lisa didn't have were the early building blocks to create confidence throughout her life, the ones described earlier in the chapter. Lisa's parents didn't support her interests, nor did they provide what she needed to feel cared for and valued. Lisa and her brother were left to their own devices, leaving Lisa with the feeling that she was not important. When she had an opportunity to go the extra mile (the tutoring), her mother made it clear that this interest was not a priority to her. When Lisa won the French award through her own aptitude and diligence, her mother took credit for her success.

The voice that lingers inside Lisa says: *Even when I work hard, maybe it doesn't count. Maybe I didn't earn it. Bottom line: I can't trust myself. And what I think or need doesn't really matter anyway.* How did Lisa, and how can you, learn to develop the building blocks of confidence when the groundwork wasn't laid down for you growing up?

This is a good time to take out your notebook. Please give yourself quiet time to reflect on the following questions, knowing they might bring up challenging thoughts, emotions, or memories. It can help to review the practices you have learned so far in this book to handle upsetting emotions, such as deep breathing, grounding with five senses, and self-compassion.

- Do any of any of the experiences in the list above resonate with you?

- Which ones?

- Can you briefly write about one of those experiences?

- What thoughts, emotions, or physical sensations are you noticing as you recall this experience?

- How has that experience made you feel about yourself and your abilities?

- How has that experience, or others like that, impacted how you think, feel, or act in the present?

- Knowing what you know now about your mother, how would you like to feel about this situation? Yourself and your abilities? Your mother's actions?

These questions help you rewrite the story, or voice, that plays in your head, to connect the dots in a different way. Through answering these questions, Lisa realized that every time she questioned one of her parenting decisions, the emotions she felt reminded her of when those feelings of "I don't matter" came up, as they had when she was hanging out drinking with her friends as a teenager. Back then, part of her was having fun. However, part of her teenage self felt that if she mattered more, her parents would spend time with her and pay attention to what she was up to.

The burning in her stomach reminded her, deep inside, of how she felt when her mother stole the show at graduation (and other times), negating Lisa's hard work and accomplishments. Lisa realized that her mother's behavior, as awful as it felt to Lisa, was not about her. It was about her mother's inability to care for her and value her. The more Lisa wrote about this in her journal, the more clearly she saw this reality. With practice, Lisa learned to step back from her mother's voice and tune in to her own. Another important part of building confidence is identifying your strengths, and in the next section, we'll explore that.

The Significance of Strengths

What are you good at? What do you like? Being able to identify your strengths is a cousin to knowing what you value but with a different spin. Values are what's important to you, the guiding lights that shape your decisions and actions.

Your strengths are aspects of your character, like those puzzle pieces of a personality. Your character or personality strengths are "the positive parts of your personality that make you feel authentic and engaged" (Via Institute on Character n.d.). In this way, your character strengths go hand in hand with your values. For example, let's say one of your character strengths is perseverance and one of your values is contributing to your community. Your ability to stick with things and your value of contributing might work together when you're feeling tired and nonetheless you show up for your shift at the food pantry. But first you have to know how to identify your strengths.

Why You Struggle with Spotting Your Strengths

Growing up, you learn about your strengths in several ways. First, simply by having the experience of being loved, cherished, and "seen" by your parent. The experience of emotional security and being valued for who you are sets the stage for feeling you can go out in the world and try new things. Second, you learn by doing. You need the opportunity to try, fail, and pick yourself up knowing you are loved all along. As the daughter of a narcissistic mother, it's unlikely you felt this way very often.

Gemma, age twenty-seven, is first-generation Korean American. Growing up, Gemma struggled in school. She was quiet by nature and preferred art to academics. She had one best friend, a "quirky" boy named Oliver. Gemma tried to spend as much time as possible at Oliver's house. When she was home, her mother's criticism was nonstop. Gemma was expected to excel at school and gain entrance to a prestigious university. But when Gemma tried to sit at her desk for hours on end, her mind drifted. She wanted to be outside or do her art projects.

When Gemma entered middle school, her enraged mother insisted it was not appropriate for her to spend so much time at a boy's house. She insisted Gemma come home after school. Gemma grew lonelier and lonelier.

Gemma now lives at home with her parents. She graduated from high school and took a few courses at community college. But Gemma has never been able to find her way. She earns money doing data entry from home. One night, Gemma's parents came home after an evening out and found that Gemma had taken an overdose of ibuprofen. The emergency department doctor referred Gemma to a therapist. Her mother was furious, claiming that Gemma shamed the family. But Gemma started therapy anyway.

Gemma's parents emigrated to the United States from Korea in the 1980s, bringing their professional skills, status, and plans to start a family. They settled in New York City, where they had Gemma and her younger brother, Harry. Both Gemma and Harry were held to high academic standards. Anything below an A was unacceptable.

However, for Gemma's mother, her appearance and behavior were on her report card too. Harry could hang out late with his friends, get drunk, and do drugs. He was the prince. But Gemma knew she was never good enough, let alone could ever get away with Harry's "extracurricular activities."

Gemma loved to go outside and draw, but her mother forbid it because pale skin was highly valued in traditional Korean culture. "How will you be successful with dark skin?" she taunted, refusing to let Gemma out on weekends while Harry lounged by the pool. When Gemma pointed out her art teachers' praise, her mother replied: "I was top of my class. I won every award."

After Gemma graduated from high school, her mother insisted she get plastic surgery to narrow her jaw, a common procedure in Korea. When Gemma balked, her mother snapped: "You don't have a choice if you ever want to get married." Gemma went ahead with the procedure. Gemma knows that some of her Korean American friends felt good about having their noses narrowed or eyelids reshaped, but she didn't. Gemma was shocked to learn that some of her friends were also allowed by their parents to forgo the procedures.

"I knew trying to get my mother to listen to me was hopeless. And my father went along, like he was afraid of her."

Gemma was able to untangle her experiences little by little in therapy. Gemma's upbringing was influenced by her family's cultural norms. But for Gemma, the traditional Korean values of high academic performance, gender expectations, and even looking a certain way were intensified by her mother's narcissistic traits and behaviors.

Once she started therapy, Gemma was identified with a learning difference, which helped her understand her struggle in school. This knowledge emboldened Gemma to take some art classes and train to become a graphic designer. Gemma learned that her mother's cruel behavior was not part of being Korean, and it was not Gemma's fault. Most importantly, Gemma learned that she could not change her mother or ever make her learn to value her. Over time, Gemma earned a certificate in graphic design and moved into her own apartment. She created her own life and learned to listen to her own voice.

Next, you'll learn how to identify your strengths. This exercise is based on the field of positive psychology. Researchers Christopher Peterson and Martin Seligman (2004) identified twenty-four character strengths found in adults across the United States and around the world, regardless of culture. More importantly, Seligman's team (2005) studied exercises that help people feel more positive in their lives by tapping into their identified strengths.

Practice: Spotting Your Strengths

Here is a modified list of the original strengths and virtues found in the research I just mentioned. Please look at the list and in your journal, write down the ones you feel apply to you most strongly. Note that the twenty-four strengths fall into six main categories (Via Institute on Character, n.d.).

Wisdom

You are a creative problem solver.

You are curious—interested in new things and open to new ideas.

You use your judgment: you think things through.

You love learning and mastering new skills.

You offer wise advice to others and take the "big picture" view.

Courage

You are brave. You speak up for what is right.

You work hard and finish what you start.

You are honest, trustworthy, and sincere.

You are enthusiastic and energetic and put your whole heart into things.

Humanity

You are warm and genuine and value close relationships.

You are compassionate and caring.

You understand the feelings of others.

Justice

You are loyal, a team player.

You play fair.

You don't let preconceptions of others influence your decisions.

You are a leader, encouraging groups to get things done.

Temperance

You are forgiving. You accept people's shortcomings and give second chances.

You are modest, letting your accomplishments speak for themselves.

You are careful, cautious, and don't take undue risks.

You manage your emotions and impulses.

Transcendence

You appreciate beauty and excellence and feel inspired by the goodness of others.

You feel thankful for good things and express that thanks.

You have a sense of humor. You can be playful and lighthearted.

You feel a sense of purpose and spirituality.

Now that you have identified your strengths, you can use these strengths to increase your confidence and well-being. Here's how (Seligman et al. 2005).

1. Use one of your strengths in a new and different way every day for one week. Let's say one of your strengths is *love of learning*. You stay late at work every night because there are so many changes in the computer system and you enjoy being on top of things. Plus, when you were growing up, your mother pitted you and your siblings against each other. You could never live up to your high-achieving brother and sisters. You're starting to realize you do everything you can to push that voice away, at the cost of yourself. The one that says: "You'll never measure up."

Practice taking small steps to build confidence and the sense of mastery you read about earlier in the chapter. Say you love to garden, but there's not enough time to dig into your hobby because you get home from work so late. This week you leave work on time. You read up on bulbs. You go to the garden center, buy the bulbs, and plant them where they will get the right amount of sun. You'll see what grows.

2. For one week, write down three things that went well each day, including the cause(s) for what went well. Take Gemma from earlier in this chapter. Gemma noticed that her graphic design professor complimented her project, on which she had worked very hard. She noted that she succeeded on the project because of two of her strengths: she *appreciated beauty* and was *persistent*. Gemma also noticed that she was able to ignore an unkind comment her mother made about her appearance instead of taking it to heart and feeling sad. Gemma recognized that she was able to do this because she was *aware of what makes her mother tick*. As such, Gemma knew her mother's comment about Gemma's appearance was about her insecurity, and Gemma could step back from it and focus on what was important to her.

3. Ask other people who know you well to write stories about specific situations in which you were at your best. Although this may be difficult for you, ask the writers to incorporate as many details as possible. Read and examine these stories for themes indicating your strengths. Research found that asking other people to reflect on your strengths and write about them in detail helps in multiple ways (Roberts et al. 2005). Studies indicate this process strengthens the immune system, decreases the body's reaction to stress, and increases creative problem-solving ability (Lee, Cable, and Staats 2017). It also increases healthy emotions and the feeling that you can make changes in your life (Roberts, Heaphy, and Caza 2019).

Lisa, from earlier in this chapter, reviewed her stories for themes and found that people valued her *courage, kindness, and awareness of others' feelings*. Lisa decided that as much as she loved being home with her children, she needed something for herself. She started taking one class at a time to become a therapist, a dream that had long been at the back of her mind.

Savoring Your Strengths

What did it feel like to identify your strengths? Many daughters of narcissistic mothers feel uncomfortable acknowledging parts of themselves they feel proud of. Perhaps that "Who am I?" voice came up. Perhaps you weren't sure what your strengths are. Whatever you are feeling, remember to offer yourself compassion. It gets easier with practice, time, and patience. You have the right to feel good about yourself, to try, to make mistakes, and to try again. Even if it doesn't always please other people.

In this chapter, you learned that confidence is both the feeling of self-assurance and the belief that you can persist in the face of challenges. You learned to identify your strengths and how to build them to grow your confidence and well-being. With this foundation, you can move on to the next chapter, in which you'll learn how to set boundaries and communicate assertively.

Chapter 9

Building Boundaries and Becoming Assertive

Boundaries are our unique set of *internal rules* about what we will and won't do. Our boundaries also define what is acceptable, or not, in terms of how other people treat us. Boundaries are based on our values and needs. They fall into these domains: time, physical, emotional and mental, religious and spiritual, and financial and material (Martin 2021). Here are examples of an overridden boundary in each of those domains.

Time. Your next-door neighbor calls and says breathlessly, "Can you pick up the kids from the bus stop and keep them until I get home from work? A big project is taking longer than I expected." This is starting to be routine. But you want to be a good person, so you say yes, even though you wanted quiet time at home with your own children that afternoon. The next few times you see her name on your caller ID, you don't answer the phone. But now, when you see her on walks around the neighborhood, you feel uncomfortable and try to avoid her.

Physical. When your in-laws visit, they refuse to wear masks. Your husband explains: "This is how they are." It makes you extremely uncomfortable, to say the least. Your husband doesn't want to rock the boat, and you argue about it each time before they visit. This time when your in-laws show up, you hand them masks at the door and storm upstairs. The kids cry. Your husband is angry. Your in-laws leave in a huff.

Emotional and mental. You're out to lunch with a group of friends, and one of them brings up something you thought you shared with her in confidence. The next thing you know, everyone is talking about this subject and giving you "advice." You stay silent because you don't want to offend your friend or create "drama."

Religious and spiritual. You're a practicing Muslim. As such, you don't drink alcohol. At the office holiday party, you explain this to your colleague, who says: "Oh, c'mon, it's Christmas! Live a little!" You feel angry and embarrassed. You wish you knew what to say to guys like this instead of just feeling stuck.

Sexual. Your ex calls every few months to hook up. You feel awful afterward and tell yourself you'll say no next time he calls. But then you think it will be different this time, and he will really want to get back together. You don't trust your better judgment.

Financial and material. Your brother has struggled with drugs for years. He's been in and out of rehab and sober houses. It's painful to see him suffering. He's texted you at work, asking for rent money. You can't bear to let him live on the street, but you've learned enough that you don't let him live with you. So you give him the money.

Boundaries are like the painted lines on the roads that separate the lanes. Often, we don't pay much attention to them when we drive. But what would happen if we didn't have those lines? Chaos and danger. We need lines, or boundaries, to keep us safe, to guide us, and to remind us that we are separate from other people, even as we coexist. This is especially true when situations are challenging, conflictual, or just unclear. Have you ever driven on a foggy, rainy night when you can barely see an inch in front of you? Perhaps you're hunched over the steering wheel, squeezing it until your hands hurt, sweat trickling down your face. Perhaps your eyes are focused on the lines on the road, the only things guiding you safely to your destination. Like those illuminated lines, your boundaries guide you in the right direction.

You may think of additional categories of boundaries that are relevant to you. Here is what all types of boundaries have in common: they require you to know what you feel and think; to value, respect, and manage your own thoughts and feelings; and when necessary, to take action on your thoughts and feelings even if you feel those actions might not be well-received by someone else. This is not easy, especially for daughters of narcissistic mothers.

Why You Struggle to Set Boundaries

The emotional security that's required to set boundaries is not laid down in daughters who grew up in families with narcissism. The good news is, setting boundaries is a skill that can be learned, and we'll talk about that later in this chapter. Boundary setting is a skill that goes hand in hand with assertiveness skills, and we'll talk about those too.

Here are examples that illustrate factors you may have experienced growing up that contribute to your difficulty setting boundaries.

Jamie: "My mother used to come into my room whenever she felt like it, even when I was a teenager. When I saw that she read my diary, I flipped out. She told me I was 'over dramatic' and that anything in my room belonged to her because it was her house. It's hard to shake the feeling that I have no rights."

Brittany: "My mother did not get along with her own mother, who lived next door to us. All day long, they were on the phone, fighting. Then my mother would complain to me about how terrible my grandmother was and how miserable she made her. It didn't seem to matter what I felt or what was going on my life. I just had to sit and listen or she would accuse me of not caring about her either. I really want to stop people-pleasing. I know I could never make my mother happy. It wasn't my job. "

Aimee: "My mother didn't believe in doctors. It wasn't a religious thing. She just didn't trust them and thought she knew better. When I was in the eighth grade, I really didn't feel well for several months. I was tired all the time. I had no energy. I told my mother, but she told me to spend more time outside. The worse I felt, the more she made she feel it was my fault, like I was just lazy. One day, I fainted at school. The school nurse said I had to have a doctor's note before I could come back. It turned out I was severely anemic. You'd think I'd be great at self-care now. But I still try to tough it out. It's hard for me to take how I feel seriously, as if I don't deserve it."

What do these stories illustrate? As the daughter of a narcissistic mother, you likely grew up feeling that you had no right to privacy, no right to say no, you were not entitled to your feelings, or were responsible for other people's feelings and it was your job to make other people happy (Donaldson-Pressman and Pressman 1994).

These factors muddied the water, so it's hard to see yourself clearly now that you are an adult (What do you think, feel, and need?). In addition, your experiences growing up made it hard to see other people clearly as well. Although your mother was unable to respect your feelings or see you as a separate person from herself, other people can do that when you express what you want and need clearly and with conviction.

Now it's your turn to identify the types of boundaries you struggle with. This is a good time to get out your journal and respond to the following prompts. You might not struggle in all areas. It also helps to connect the dots, to decipher which early experiences are behind your shaky boundaries. As always, be aware of the thoughts, emotions, memories, or physical sensations that arise and what you have learned so far that helps you: deep breathing, mindfulness, self-compassion.

- A time my boundary was crossed was when…

- When this happened, I felt…

- When this happened, I thought…

- When this happened, I… [action you took or didn't take]

- This is important to me because…

- This situation reminds me of earlier in my life when…

- If I had a "redo," I would…

This type of boundary was (circle): time, physical, emotional and mental, religious and spiritual, sexual, financial and material.

It's also important to understand when you feel more confident setting boundaries. To help you do that, write your answers for the following set of prompts in your journal.

- A time I held my boundary was when…

- When this happened, I felt…

- When this happened, I thought…

- When this happened I… [action you took or didn't take]

- This is important to me because…

- This situation reminds me of earlier in my life when…

- If I had a "redo," I would…

This type of boundary was (circle): time, physical, emotional and mental, religious and spiritual, sexual, financial and material.

Note: If you want to print out these questions, download the Types of Boundaries worksheet at http://www.newharbinger.com/50096. Feel free to complete it as many times as would be helpful to you. This will help clarify which types of boundaries are more challenging for you and which you feel more confident with. Next, you'll learn practices that help you stand up for what you think, feel, and want.

Building Boundaries

Throughout this book, you've practiced identifying your emotions and values. You've learned that when you feel overwhelmed by strong emotions, you can ground yourself with your five senses and breathe slowly and deeply. You've practiced managing perfectionism and worried thoughts. You've learned that although you did not grow up with your mother's empathy for your emotions, you can calm and heal yourself with self-compassion. Now, you can bring all these practices together as you learn to stand up for yourself in ways small and large.

Setting boundaries could be defined as "standing firm." Mountain Pose, or Tadasana, is one of yoga's standing poses and one that most people can do comfortably. Practicing Mountain Pose helps you feel strong, solid, and well, like a mountain. Research indicates that practicing Mountain Pose for only two minutes increased feelings of self-esteem, energy, being in control, and empowerment (Golec de Zavala, Lantos, and Bowden 2017). If you have any concerns about your balance, please practice near a wall or counter. Also, make sure to stand with your feet hip distance apart to give you a steady base (McCall 2007).

Practice: Mountain Pose

The good news is you don't have to be a yoga guru to practice Mountain Pose. You can try the steps below and see how you feel. You can also find instructions for Mountain Pose on YouTube. It can help to practice regularly to get the hang of it. Then, you can try it out before setting a boundary with someone. See what happens!

1. Stand upright with your feet parallel, about hip distance apart. *Keeping your feet hip distance apart helps you maintain balance. This is especially important if you are new to yoga or this pose.*

2. Balance your weight evenly across your feet. Keep your knees soft, not locked.

3. Lift the top of your chest toward the ceiling and open your collarbone area. Keep your shoulders open and down, away from your ears.

4. Press your feet firmly into the floor. Be aware and mindful of your muscles throughout your body. Hold them with strength and energy but without straining.

Now you have a way to use your body to help you physically feel more adept at setting boundaries. To start setting boundaries in your life, you will take action based on what's important to you. You know that, as the daughter of a narcissistic mother, you may have made choices based on feeling unworthy, ashamed, anxious, or invisible. As you identified in the boundary-setting journal exercise, that doesn't mean you live that way in all areas of your life. You can use your identified values to begin practicing boundary setting in certain areas of your life, starting with one small step.

Practice: One Small Step

In this practice, you'll create a plan to change your patterns. This is a learning process, which you'll change and adapt as you determine what works best for you in different situations. Below are the steps.

1. What's your "why"?
What is an area of life that you value in which you want to feel more competent setting boundaries? For example, you might value contributing to others, having fun, or standing up for yourself. In your journal, write down one value.

2. What's your "how"?
Identify one *small* step you can take to enact a boundary in this area and bring it to life. Write it down in your journal, describing how you will do it.

For example, if you value contributing to others, you might decide you want to volunteer one Saturday afternoon per month, even if it means asking your partner to do the grocery shopping. If you value having fun, maybe you will meet a friend for a dinner, even if means experiencing the anxiety of not checking off everything on your to-do list at work. If you value protecting your family, it might look like telling your mother you will not answer questions about your son's college applications. Remember that your step can be as small as you need it to be. Your journey of change is a marathon (in a good way!), not a sprint.

The One Small Step practice is like the process of exposure therapy for anxiety disorders. With exposure therapy, people face their fears gradually, learning that they can handle their uncomfortable thoughts, emotions, and sensations in their body. That doesn't mean those thoughts and feelings go away, but that people can move toward what's important to them in the face of discomfort.

Elements of Exposure

You can apply the principles of exposure therapy to practicing boundary setting. Remember the woman from earlier in the chapter who wanted to stop taking care of her neighbor's children after school? First, she had to practice feeling uncomfortable. It's human nature to want to get rid of uncomfortable feelings. With boundary setting, that could mean saying yes when you want to say no. It could be saying no when you feel compelled or obligated to say yes.

You can practice feeling uncomfortable and handling the urge to get rid of the discomfort in the tiniest of ways. For example, wear your shoes on the opposite feet, your watch on the opposite wrist, your shirt backward, your hair down instead of up or vice versa, or hold your fork or toothbrush with your nondominant hand. Sound crazy? Try it and see. Changing things up like this will feel uncomfortable. You'll have the urge to switch back to how you regularly do things. Instead, notice what it feels like and stick with it. Allow the urge to pass. You'll build the muscle of "getting comfortable being uncomfortable," the foundation for boundary setting.

Get the picture? Boundary setting involves changing how we approach other people or our own internal emotions. You might have to make a request of or set a limit with someone else. In contrast, you might have to set a boundary with yourself. In that sense, boundary setting is a form of self-care. Write about this in your journal by answering the following questions.

- What is your small step?

- What might come up inside you as you take on this small step?

- What thoughts, emotions, memories, or physical sensations might arise? Can you connect the dots to earlier experiences?

Assertiveness Analysis

Assertiveness skills are the partner to boundary-setting skills. Here are examples of what life is like without them.

You can still hear inside your mind asking your college roommate to do her dishes, the ones piling up in the sink for a week. The walls in the dorm are so thin! You overheard her telling her boyfriend how annoying and "OCD" you were. So for the rest of the year, you did her dishes yourself.

You run an established home renovation business. Not many women succeed in the world of construction. It's a man's gig, and you're proud of yourself. So why do you let your clients walk all over you? This week, one client insisted on changing out her kitchen cabinets at the last minute, insisting she had "no idea" a fee was involved in a late switch. You don't want to antagonize her, so you waive the fee. And anyway, you wonder: Did you remind her when she signed the contract? Maybe it's your fault.

You ordered your burger without onions. You were very clear about this because you are allergic to them. But there are rings of red onions on your plate. You're tired of not being taken seriously You charge right up to the hostess, even though there is a long line, and in a loud voice demand a refund.

What themes do you see in these examples?

- "My feelings don't count. They're stupid. Who am I to ask for something?"
- "I can't trust my own abilities or perceptions."
- "I have no value."
- "Other people's needs are more important than mine."
- "My needs are just trouble."
- "You have to get in someone's face to get anywhere."

Do any of those themes sound familiar to you? It's not easy to be asser-tive, especially for women. Multiple research studies, not to mention what you read in the news every day, make clear that women are more likely than men to be interrupted, to be underrepresented on conference panels, and to be penalized for speaking out at work (Porges 2020). In fact, there is even a term for these male-dominated panels: "manels"!

On top of it, if you are raised by a narcissistic mother, you come to the assertiveness table with an even less favorable hand of cards. At least three main factors from your upbringing contribute to your difficulty asking for what you need. First, there is gaslighting. If your mother caused you to doubt your sense of reality and to doubt your own feelings, it's not surpris-ing that as an adult you would question what you want or that you have a right to ask for it.

Second, there is emotional invalidation. If your mother ignored, put down, or even mocked your emotions, it's not surprising that you would do the same to yourself. Asking for what you want in a clear, respectful way requires the ability to respect yourself. It also helps to have had this behav-ior modeled for you.

Third, there is emotion dysregulation. Depending on where they are on the narcissistic spectrum, narcissistic mothers have little, sporadic, or no insight into their emotions or capacity to manage them in appropriate ways. As such, maybe your mother flew into a rage when you didn't get into your first-choice college, which is also her alma mater to which she has donated a great deal of money. Maybe she called the admissions director and demanded to know why and that you get to interview again because you had a cold that day. You asked her not to call the director, but she told you it was "not your business." After your mother's showdown, you were never sure if you got off the wait list because of her tantrum or because you deserved it. On the other side of the coin, you too might have the tendency to take an aggressive stance when trying to get your needs met since this is what you saw growing up. This method often backfires, leaving you feeling frustrated, incompetent, unfairly treated, or angrier.

When Rebecca graduated from her cosmetology program, she rented a chair at a hair salon. She developed a loyal clientele and prided herself on taking ongoing classes to learn new techniques for cutting and coloring. One Saturday afternoon, her childhood friend, Chloe, dropped by the salon, expecting her usual free haircut and blowout. Rebecca was on a brief break, between doing hair for two large wedding parties. Nonetheless, she did Chloe's hair, gulping down her lunch in between snips.

"I was always good at doing hair," Chloe announced, twirling in front of the mirror after Rebecca removed her cape. "Everybody said so. I didn't need to go to beauty school." Part of Rebecca felt angry and humiliated. Part of her felt guilty. Shouldn't she make time for Chloe? But she was sick of this. She had her own life too.

Rebecca was raised by Doris, who left Rebecca with the feeling that she was always "in trouble." Doris expected Rebecca and her younger brother to clean the house, cook dinner, and walk the dog while she was at work. Rebecca knew she should help her single mother, but she never did things right. When Rebecca's brother developed asthma, she made sure that his inhaler always had refills. As an adult, Rebecca feels guilty and unsure about herself because she was not able to see that the task of pleasing her mother was impossible.

Being raised by Doris was like trying to blow out a trick party candle. You blow, and the flame pops right back. If you don't know it's a party trick, then you'll probably think, *There's something wrong with me.* As Rebecca learned to understand her relationship with her mother and how it impacted her, she learned to stand up for herself. Eventually, Rebecca felt confident enough to open her own salon, which required her to be clear and straightforward with employees, vendors, landlord, and clients, to name of a few of the people she interacted with. She told Chloe that she couldn't show up for free haircuts anymore and she could call for an appointment.

Achieving Assertiveness

Although being assertive is often difficult to do, the concept is straightforward. When you're assertive, you say what think, feel, or want in a way that is respectful of other people's feelings and rights. Unfortunately, being assertive is often confused with being aggressive, controlling, and hostile. However, done "right," assertive communication is direct, honest, and specific (Pfafman 2017). That's it. Like everything you are learning in this book, assertiveness is a skill that takes practice. Next, let's talk about what you need to know to practice assertive behavior with some basic *do* and *don't* guidelines.

Do:

- Decide in advance what your goal or need is. What do you want to get out of a conversation? Be specific.

- Let the other person know that you want to have a conversation.

- Use "I" language to express your feelings and concerns.

- Listen to the other person with empathy.

Here's how this plays out for Rebecca. Rebecca's goal: Have people respect my time. "Chloe, it's very hard when you come without an appointment. I feel frustrated and that my time is not valuable."

Then, make your request for change. Again, use "I" language. "From now on, I would like you to call in advance to schedule a hair appointment when it is convenient for me."

Remember that Rome wasn't built in a day. If a conversation is not going well or you feel rattled, take a break. You can come back to it. Say something like: "I'd like to take a break and come back to this conversation when we are both calmer. I will contact you about a good time."

Don't:

- Apologize for your needs, wants, or requests.

- Issue orders.

- Make it personal. "You are so inconsiderate."

- Threaten the other person.

You may be thinking: *Easier said than done!* If so, here is a tip to help you stay on track. Assertiveness can be boiled down to the three Cs: calm, clear, and congenial.

Calm. You may feel anxious when you assert yourself. How do you handle your strong emotions so they don't overtake you and prevent you from moving forward? The practice, "emotion surfing," is based on the idea that our emotions are like waves. All waves rise, peak, and subside. No wave, no matter how high, stays at its peak forever. It always flows out to shore.

Exercise: Emotion Surfing for Calm

Emotion surfing is based on the idea of "urge surfing," a concept developed by addiction psychologist Alan Marlatt in the 1980s to help people manage their urges for addictive substances (Larimer et al. 1999). When you feel overwhelmed by anxiety, fear, or anger, it might help to know that your emotions are powerful urges as well and that they can be tolerated. Here are the steps to practice emotion surfing:

1. What do you notice in your body right now? Describe the sensations as clearly as possible, for example: tingling in your fingers, tightness in your neck, sweaty palms.

2. What are you feeling right now (emotions)? Sadness, anger, excitement, worry, disgust, relief?

3. What are your thoughts? Can you notice them and let them go, like placing them on leaves on a stream?

4. How "high" is your emotional wave now, on a scale of 0 to 10?

5. Can you identify the strongest emotion and where it is in your body?

6. Can you soften into that part of your body and allow that emotion to be there?

7. Can you talk kindly to yourself about how you are feeling, like you would to a good friend?

8. How strong is the emotion now on the scale of 0 to 10?

Repeat as often as you need to until the wave is at a level that feels comfortable to you.

Clear. Being clear means using simple, straightforward language. Get straight to the point. Avoid language such as, "I guess," "I'm not sure," "I just," "This might not be right..." Instead, use strong vocabulary, such as "I would like," "I need," "I am uncomfortable..." (Mindell 2001).

Congenial. Being congenial means paying attention to your tone of voice and body language, two key components of successful communication. Speak in a clear, steady voice. Make eye contact. Do your best to keep your body relaxed and open.

Your Sticking Points

As we've discussed, being assertive does not come naturally for many people, especially women. Now, let's look at particular sticking points for daughters of narcissistic mothers. Being assertive means expressing your feelings and ideas and making requests of other people. It doesn't mean other people are going to like your assertive behavior or react well! You may find that people, for their own reasons, do any of the following things: change the subject, get angry, make fun of you, try to make you feel guilty, criticize you, tell you your request has no merit, or try to throw you off guard by questioning why you want what you want (Bourne 1995). In turn, you might be especially vulnerable to questioning yourself. You might be vulnerable to slipping into feelings of shame and self-doubt.

So what can you do? First remember, you have many practices to help you. Go back to your values. What matters to you, deep inside, prompting you to make this request? Have there been times in the past when you have stood up for yourself in a way you felt good about? How did you do that? What does that say about your strengths and resources? Can you talk to yourself with kindness and compassion?

In this chapter, you have learned about the importance of setting boundaries and being assertive and why this can be a struggle for you. You've learned ways to practice these important skills. These skills will be especially important for the issues you'll learn about in the next chapter: your relationships with your siblings.

Chapter 10

Relationships and Creating Your Life

This chapter addresses one of the most sensitive issues for daughters of narcissistic mothers: being a sibling and your relationships with your siblings. You may experience some of the following common relationship patterns.

- Do you struggle to communicate directly with people? Do you find it easier to talk "through" somebody else, like a game of telephone?

- Do you feel anxious in relationships, uncertain about your value or ability to hold onto love and connection?

- Do you feel "less than" other people, constantly doubting and second-guessing yourself?

- Do you find it hard to trust other people, even those close to you?

- Do you have few memories from growing up? Does your childhood seem like a blur?

If you do, you are not alone as these are common experiences in daughters.

Sibling Styles

Next, we'll look at patterns in families with narcissistic mothers. We'll look at how these patterns impact how you feel, think, and act as an adult. Below are three ways family dynamics play out with a narcissistic mother.

Birds of a Feather Flock Together

In this dynamic, you and your siblings are close. That doesn't mean you always get along perfectly or agree on everything. Would you have picked growing up with a narcissistic mother if you had a choice? No way. But you came through your childhood feeling like a team. You have inside jokes. You have inside pain too. Sometimes it's hard for other people to understand the situation with your mother the way you and your siblings do, even your partners or close friends. That can be tough.

Maybe you and your siblings text or talk all the time, sharing every update or annoyance about Mom. Maybe you support each other about how to handle the holidays or Mom's health care. Mostly, within this little circle, you feel understood and sure of yourself. If only that feeling translated into the rest of the world.

Divided We Fall

Growing up, only one kid in your family got your mother's approval, and you were not it if this was your family dynamic. You're still trying to figure yourself out, still finding your way in life. You and your siblings barely speak if you speak at all. When you do, the interactions are cold or cutting. Looking back, it's no wonder. Growing up in your family was like living in an episode of *Survivor*. The goal was to get through and get off the island alive.

As an adult, you try hard to do everything perfectly. You take on more than you can handle and often feel overwhelmed. When you were growing up, one way to keep your mother happy and get some attention was to keep your head down, work, and succeed. Now, you're like a hamster on a wheel, and you can't get off. Maybe you gave up trying to please your mother. There was no point.

Flying Solo

In a family with this dynamic, you feel like an outlier. Since you grew up as an only child with your narcissistic mother, there is nobody who understands your experience. Maybe there is another parent who understands, maybe not. As you got older and spent time at other people's houses, you realized there were other types of mothers, other types of families. That was eye-opening. Still, you often get overwhelmed by anxiety. It's hard to carry around this secret, bearing the burden of your mother's behavior by yourself. You feel guilty and responsible. Not just for your mother, for everything.

As you have read throughout this book, you may struggle with knowing what you feel, expressing your feelings, setting limits, and asking for what you want and need. You may struggle with self-doubt and feeling valuable to other people.

Family Patterns

Next, we'll look at other patterns that occur in families with narcissistic mothers. We'll look at how they may have impacted you and your siblings. We'll look at strategies you can use now to improve your relationships and communicate more effectively with others.

Upside-Down Family

In an emotionally healthy family, the parents meet the needs of the children as best they can. It bears repeating that parenting is not easy. In addition, we live in a culture that does not support parents with childcare or paid leave and in many other ways. However, in a family with narcissism, the children exist to meet the needs of the parents. Children learn to "read" their mother, sensing her moods and needs, trying to bolster her up or prevent her hurtful attacks.

Were you the sensitive child in the family? When you were growing up, could you sense your mother's mood the moment you stepped into the house? If you did, perhaps you tried to make her feel better; perhaps you withdrew in self-protection. Perhaps you informed your siblings, like an emergency weather report: "Tornado warning. Take shelter." How your siblings responded depended on their temperaments and personality styles. Perhaps you bonded; perhaps you had a sibling who stayed out of the house as much as possible. There is no one way things fall out in the families with a narcissistic mother.

Emotional Hot Potato

As you've learned throughout this book, your mother was likely cut off from her feelings; was sensitive to perceived criticism; had erratic, "Swiss cheese" empathy; and had little or no insight into how her behavior impacted you or other people.

In addition, your mother likely engaged in "emotional hot potato" (also known as "projection" in the mental health world). Here's how it works. Your brother Joe (the favorite child) and his wife, Rachel, ask Rachel's parents to babysit their children while they go away for a long weekend. Your mother is jealous and enraged. However, she can't admit to those feelings to herself or others. That would mean getting angry at her favorite child or wondering why the in-laws were chosen over her. Instead, her feelings of jealousy and rage are like hot potatoes in her hands. They burn! She can't hold onto them. So she throws them straight to you. And then you catch these painful feelings, like an expert Major League Baseball player. A conversation with your mother might sound like this:

You: That looks like a beautiful condo Joe and Rachel rented for the weekend.

Mom: Are you jealous? You were always jealous of Joe. Why can't you just be happy for them?

You can probably see how emotional hot potato feels a lot like gaslighting as well. You might feel crazy, doubt your perception of reality, and worst of all, doubt who you are as a person. Are you a jealous person who can't be happy for your brother? That feels awful.

Do you have a solid relationship with Joe? If so, the relationship and how you see yourself can withstand your narcissistic mother throwing you the hot potato. You and Joe might even laugh about it. If the relationship is damaged and shaky, then this behavior can further divide you. And that hot potato your mother couldn't stand to hold? You're stuck with it.

In addition, the conversation pushes those emotional "preset buttons" on the car radio that we discussed earlier. What thoughts, feelings, urges, or memories turn on? What buttons have been pressed? Perhaps the "I'm selfish" button or "I'm a bad person" button or "Not being seen" button.

What happens after your button is pushed? Do you notice those feelings, become willing to accept them, and do something that aligns with your values, even if those feelings are still there?

Splitting

Does your mother see you and your siblings in black-and-white categories, with no shades of gray? It's as if she does not see you as full people with all your strengths, weaknesses, likes, dislikes, goals, and dreams. Certainly, it's not unusual in families to label their children: the smart one, the funny one, the athletic one. This type of labeling is never helpful for children. However, in the world of narcissistic mothers, it's taken to extremes.

Let's think back to chapters 2 and 3 when you learned about the psychological makeup of narcissistic mothers. You learned that although your mother looks like an adult on the outside, inside she is emotionally immature, like a child. Part of becoming an adult means understanding that people:

- have negative and positive qualities

- do things we don't like sometimes, even our loved ones

- can have positive and negative qualities and still be loveable

- can have positive and negative feelings toward *themselves* and still value themselves

Your narcissistic mother struggled to do any of the above. What did that mean for you and your siblings? Maybe you are a "good" person, and your sister is 'bad." Or vice versa. If you and your siblings were "split" this way when you were growing up, these labels may have stuck inside you, impacting how you feel about yourself and your sister. The splitting you experienced in your family may also impact how you see yourself and others. Remember "if you make a mistake, you are a mistake"?

For example, Michaela is extroverted and lively, like her father, who left her mother when Michaela was six years old. Her older brother, Tom, is quiet and introverted, like her mother, Jean. Michaela recalls Jean constantly criticizing her for wanting to spend time with her friends, go to camp, or sing in the acapella group. As an adult, Michaela could recognize that her "get out there" attitude toward life reminded Jean of her ex-husband, although she never actually mentioned him. But growing up, Michaela struggled between wanting to be herself and feeling bad for not staying home like her brother. As adults, Michaela and Tom rarely see or talk to each other, even though they both work in technology and share common interests.

Secrecy

Was your family motto something like:

- *Nobody needs to know our business.*

- *What we talk about in our family stays behind closed doors.*

- *That's nobody's business!*

- *Out of sight, out of mind.*

Perhaps these mottoes were directly spoken. Perhaps they were the unspoken rules. Either way, you and your siblings learned that what mattered in your family was how things looked on the outside, to other people. What didn't matter was how you felt on the inside, what you really needed, or whether you were actually thriving in life.

Perhaps you and your siblings all got the memo on this motto, and it "helped" you become "birds of a feather who flock together." Perhaps not all of you agreed to keep the family secrets, and divided you fell. Perhaps you were an only child, and it was left to you hold the secrets and whether or not to share them.

In all these scenarios, you might be left with feelings of shame and isolation. It might be hard to trust other people. It might be hard to let anyone know who you really are and to feel truly connected. You are always protecting one family secret or another.

Olivia grew up with two parents with narcissistic traits and behaviors. She and her brothers never told anyone that her parents would leave them home alone for days while they would travel for business when Olivia and her brothers were in high school. Her parents never told them to keep quiet, but the message was clear: "Take care of yourselves." Olivia took care of her brothers, and they learned to take care of each other too. It was scary and lonely sometimes, such as the time Luke, the youngest, got hit with a baseball. Olivia called a taxi and took him to the doctor, bluffing her way through the visit. As adults, Olivia and her brothers are each other's closest friends. However, none of them have a life partner; they feel no one will ever understand each other like they do.

The Upshot for You and Your Siblings

Because of your mother's intense self-focus, there was little or no focus on building your family as a whole—building relationships between you, your parents, and your brothers and sisters. Because you and your siblings had to meet the emotional needs of your mother, you may not have had enough emotional energy left to connect with each other. Because you lived in an upside-down family, you and your siblings focused on reading Mom's emotional temperature. Because of emotional hot potato, you needed to defend and protect yourself. You missed the chance to understand what you felt and have those feeling understood and validated. Because of splitting, you learned relationships cannot be trusted. Again, this took energy away from forming positive connections with your siblings.

This is a good time to take out your journal.

- What thoughts, emotions, urges, or memories came up for you as you read?

- Which pattern(s) could you identify with?

- Which sibling style is relevant to you, and what do you identify with from that style?

- Does a particular memory come to mind about your relationship with your siblings or growing up as an only child? Please write about that memory.

- Can you connect the dots between that memory and who you are now? In what ways?

- What buttons get pushed for you now as a result of these family patterns?

- How do you handle them?

- How will you handle them when you are living in ways that align with your values and strengths?

Throughout this book, you've learned about emotions. In this chapter, you learned that sometimes your mother's intolerable negative emotions were thrown to you. You may still be "holding" them, so to speak, inside of you. Here is another practice, inspired by the tug-of-war monster metaphor used in acceptance and commitment therapy, which is based on the idea of acceptance and will help you drop that potato (Hayes, Strosahl, and Wilson 2012).

Practice: Drop the Hot Potato

Imagine you are sitting across from a figure. This figure could be real or imaginary. It could be a fictional figure from a movie, television show, or book. This figure is holding a burning, hot potato. The potato represents something that is difficult, challenging, or painful for you. Perhaps it's a negative feelings you have about yourself, a problem you can't stop worrying about, or something you feel ashamed about.

The figure tosses you the hot potato. You hold onto it tight. You grip it hard, even though it is scorching your hands. Now, your hands hurt, *and* you still have the bad feelings, worries, or shame, and no solutions.

So you decide to do something else, something new. You drop the hot potato. Just like that. You open your hands and release your grip.

Now, the potato is still there, sitting on the ground. But your hands are cooling off, little by little. Your hands are free to do what *you* want to do with them, even though the potato is still there, sitting on the ground. The figure may certainly throw another hot potato your way. That's what this figure does. And now you know you can drop it again and again, as many times as you need to, and do what's important to you.

In your journal, consider the following:

- What thoughts, emotions, urges, or memories came up as you read and experienced this exercise?

- How could this exercise help you with your concerns about your relationship with your siblings?

Earlier in this chapter, you gained clarity about growing up in an upside-down family, with emotional hot potato, splitting, and secrecy. Combined, these patterns may have made it difficult for you and your siblings to form close, trusting relationships with each other. That made it challenging for you to trust yourself and others outside the family. The following guided visualization, which is inspired by Korn and Pratt's (1990) "Mental Rehearsal: The Protective Shield" chapter in *Handbook of Hypnotic Suggestions and Metaphors*, can help you manage challenging situations and relationships in ways that feel right and comfortable to you. If you'd like to listen to this practice, you can find the recording on the website for this book, http://www.newharbinger.com/50096.

Practice: The Bubble

Please sit in a comfortable place, with your back supported. I invite you to settle into your chair and take a few deep, easy breaths. You might already begin to notice that you let go of a little more tension or stress each time you breathe out. Focus on breathing in comfort and breathing out tension.

You may notice a soothing wave of warmth flowing from your head, all the way through your body, down to your toes. Perhaps that wave has a soothing color, a color that is just right for you. Perhaps that color is flowing down from your head to your toes, bringing with it waves of comfort.

I invite you to imagine that you are surrounded by a protective bubble that only you can see. You are completely in charge of this bubble. The thing about this bubble is that it allows you to see through it and to hear whatever you choose to see and hear, while others cannot see inside the bubble. You are protected inside. You choose what comes in and out, how thick or thin the bubble is, and what can pass through it: what words, ideas, situations. It can be far away from you, or close to you.

You are in charge. You can move the bubble from place to place at any time. You are completely in control inside your bubble. You can observe and yet not take in whatever is not useful to you or in the best interest of your well-being or values.

You may be curious to notice what you discover. Your inner voice may learn something new or perhaps something you already know that is very helpful to you about yourself. And you can look out of the bubble and trust your inner voice, perhaps looking at things or yourself differently or just feeling differently.

When you are ready, take a few breaths, this time filling your body with energy. Know that you can use anything from the exercise that is valuable to you and leave behind anything that is not in your best interest or healing. You know what is right for you.

Growing Past Pain

You can grow and thrive from your struggles as the daughter of a narcissistic mother. In chapter 6, you learned that traumatic experiences get stamped in the emotional part of your brain. The impact of these memories lingers, so you react to similar situations in the present when they remind you of past traumatic events. You also learned that although memories cannot be deleted from the brain, they can be "updated" with new information so you can look at yourself, your relationships, and the world from fresh perspectives.

Mental health professionals continue to learn how people can thrive after traumatic experiences. The concept of *post-traumatic growth*, or PTG, focuses on how you can change and grow after trauma. PTG doesn't mean you're fine. It doesn't mean you don't struggle. It means that even as you struggle, you change and grow. Although it is generally looked at in terms of response to crises, such as natural disasters, assaults, or accidents, "personal growth has a common core" (Tedeschi and Calhoun 2004, 14). People can experience PTG whether or not they have experienced an acute trauma.

Let's examine how knowledge about PTG can apply to you and your relationships with your siblings. When you grow up with a narcissistic mother, there is always loss and grief. You may lose close relationships with your siblings and everything that goes with that. If you are connected, you may still feel the sense of isolation that comes from not feeling understood outside your family. You may mourn the relationship with your mother you never had. You mourn the person you could have been if things had been different when you were growing up.

You've already identified your values and strengths. Now, let's look at what values and strengths you developed *as the result* of growing up with a narcissistic mother. According to psychologist and researcher Richard Tedeschi (Joseph 2011), it's like dropping a beautiful vase, which shatters in a thousand pieces. Can you put the vase back together so it is just the same as before? No. That would be futile. However, you can turn the vase into something new and transformed. What you create from the pieces will always show the breaks, and that's okay. You're not trying to hide or cover up the damage. But something beautiful can emerge, perhaps something unexpected.

This is a good time to take out your journal. Following is a series of questions, which are organized into areas that are associated with PTG. As you consider your answers, ask yourself: Who are you as a result of being raised by a narcissistic mother? How has it shaped you in positive ways, even though you still feel pain in your life? What do you feel good about?

Appreciating Your Life

- How has your experience shaped what you value?

- How has your experience shaped how you value and appreciate yourself?

Connecting with Others

- How has your experience helped you feel that you can be close to others?

- How has your experience shaped your capacity to have empathy for others?

Seeing Possibilities in Life

- How has your experience helped you see and pursue new possibilities or opportunities in life?

- How has your experience helped you develop new interests?

Finding Your Strengths and Values

- How has your experience helped you feel that you can handle life's difficulties?

- How has your experience helped you feel that you can accept the way life works out?

Finding Meaning in Life

- How has your experience helped you find meaning in life?

- How has your experience helped you with your understanding of spiritual matters?

Remember Michaela from earlier in the chapter? She rarely saw her brother, Tom. They had little in common growing up, and their mother "split" Michaela off from the family because she could only see one part of her, the extroverted part that reminded her of Michaela's father.

As an adult, however, Michaela, came to understand that although she would always feel pain about what happened in her family, she had the strength to create something new with her brother in adulthood. Growing up, she learned that she was her own person. She could think for herself. She also learned to be compassionate toward others. She understood that Tom was quiet and unlikely to reach out to her. So she called him and invited him to dinner. Slowly, but surely, she and Tom built a relationship, first bonding over their shared work in computer programming and then their love of kayaking.

In this chapter, you learned how patterns in families with narcissistic mothers impact sibling relationships and how the ripple effects influence how you feel about yourself. You learned that in spite of these difficult experiences, you can grow and thrive. That is a great message on which to end this book as you move into the next section, "Parting Words."

Parting Words

Although this is the end of the book, I hope it is just the beginning for you, the beginning of a journey within yourself. It took courage to pick up this book, to read about your experiences, and to do the practices. I'm sure you know by now that these pages offer no quick fixes to the pain of being the daughter of a narcissistic mother because there are none. Rather, you've discovered information about yourself and practices you can use throughout your life from a place of greater self-awareness, wisdom, and self-compassion.

With any book like this, you may resonate with one part more than another. You will tap into the skills that suit you most. And that's how it should be. You are unique. After all, the goal of this book is to help you find your own voice, your authentic self. Try something every day that reminds you of who you are, what you value, and how much you're valued.

You've learned how it feels to have a narcissistic mother. You've learned what makes her tick and why it was so hard to grow up in a family with a narcissistic parent. You learned that you share many common patterns with other daughters: feelings of self-blame, shame, isolation, loneliness, and self-doubt.

Now you know that these feelings are not your fault. You can't control the thoughts and feelings that show up inside you. What a relief! But there are so many things you can do to move forward in life.

You can get to know your emotions and put words to them. You can allow your painful thoughts and feelings "to be" without having to change or control them because, well, we can't do that anyway. You can take steps to living the life that *you* want, no matter what shows up inside you. That doesn't mean being tough as nails; it's just the opposite in fact. You learned you flourish when your talk to yourself with kindness and empathy, just like you would to a good friend. In that sense, you can change the voice in your head even if you have to "change" it over and over again.

You learned you deserve to take care of yourself by setting boundaries and speaking up for your wants and needs. You can stand tall and strong, like a mountain. At the same time, like an earthquake-proof building, you are flexible. Under stress, you can bend without breaking.

I encourage you to bring these practices into your life. Not all at once, of course! Pick one thing at a time that has meaning to you and go from there. One day I was in a yoga class, and we were practicing headstand, a challenging pose for me. The teacher said: "I've been working on this pose for twenty years, and it's still hard for me." Honestly, I was floored. From my perspective, it seemed like every pose came naturally for her. It was a lightbulb moment for me.

We all have to practice, no matter what, especially things that are hard. Even if it seems like it should be easy or you should have it by now. If you grew up with a narcissistic mother, you understand that all too well. But like my yoga teacher, we all are learning, practicing, and growing. Every day.

Remember you are not alone. When feelings of self-doubt, shame, or isolation pop up in the future, please pick up this book. Dip into a section that is just right for you. Remind yourself that women around the world share your thoughts and feelings. And keep going. You are worth it.

Acknowledgments

If there's one thing that takes a village, it's writing a book. I'm so grateful to mine. I'm so grateful to Georgia Kolias, my acquisitions editor, for selecting my manuscript from the "slush pile" and believing in it all the way. Thank you to Georgia and Jennifer Holder, my development editor, whose combined editorial gifts and moral support ensured this book came to life. Thank you for teaching me how to write a book and to keep at it when my critical inner voice told me otherwise. Thank you to Gretel Hakanson, my copy editor, whose insightful work improved the manuscript in so many ways.

I'm so grateful to Wendy Behary, LCSW, narcissism expert for writing the foreword to this book. Your support means so much to me.

Thank you to the following people whose insight and professional skills were invaluable during the years I wrote this book:

Book coaches Cindy Belliveau; Lisa Tener; Matt Boone, LCSW; and the late Jeanne Ballew, without whom this book would not exist. Jeannie, I miss you and listened to your smart, encouraging voice as I worked on this book.

Kristen Meekhof, MSW, for helping me understand narcissism more deeply and teaching me how to get the word out.

The board of the New England Society for Clinical Hypnosis for teaching me so much and taking me into the fold: Lorna McKenzie-Pollock, LICSW; Rebecca Johnston, PhD; Harvey Zarren, MD; Pamela Devaney, PsyD; Russell Chin, DDS; Kaloyan Tanev, MD; Ellen Cohen, MD; Tanya Cherkerzian, LICSW; and Claire Scigliano, PsyD.

For their expertise and wisdom, which has helped me become a better therapist and author: Courtney Armstrong, MEd, LPC; Patti Ashley, PhD, LPC; Ann Brochin, PhD; Jodi Galin, PhD; Stephanie Gerber Wilson, PhD; Vita Golub-Ginsburg, LMHC; Claire M. Hart, PhD; Jonathan Inz, PhD; Bethany Montgomery, LICSW; Kimberly J. Morrow, LCSW;

Bonnie Ohye, PhD; Elsa Ronningstam, PhD; Kristen S. Springer, PhD; and Jill Stoddard, PhD.

To the Ferkauf Graduate School of Psychology of Yeshiva University, which provided a wonderful education.

For her expert website design: Stephanie Gerber Wilson, PhD.

Shannon Pallatta, graphic designer.

Lisa Mauriello, yoga teacher extraordinaire.

To my friends who keep me going and mean everything to me: my book groups and the Tuesday mahjong group, and Jodi Berenson; Caren Caplan; Marjorie Dermer, PhD; Susan Diamond; Anne Duncan, PhD; and Mary Anne Yanulis, PhD.

To the women and men who have shared their stories with me. It's my honor to work with you. You teach me so much.

To my family and to the entire Kriesberg clan. I could not have asked for a more wonderful family to marry into.

To my amazing husband, Ellis, who kept me going with his unwavering love and support. Thank you for giving me the time and space to complete this project.

To my precious daughters, Lea and Talia. I'm so proud of the independent, resilient, caring women you have become and are becoming. May you always listen to your inner voices.

References

American Psychiatric Association. 2013. *Diagnostic and Statistical Manual of Mental Disorders*, 5th ed. Arlington, VA: American Psychiatric Association.

Armstrong, C. 2015. *The Therapeutic "Aha!": 10 Strategies for Getting Your Clients Unstuck*. New York: W. W. Norton & Company.

Armstrong, C. 2019. *Rethinking Trauma Treatment: Attachment, Memory Reconsolidation, and Resilience*. New York: W. W. Norton & Company.

Ashley, P. 2020. *Shame-Informed Therapy: Treatment Strategies to Overcome Core Shame and Reconstruct the Authentic Self*. Eau Claire, WI: PESI Publishing & Media.

Baskin-Sommers, A., E. Krusemark, and E. Ronningstam. 2014. "Empathy in Narcissistic Personality Disorder: From Clinical and Empirical Perspectives." *Personality Disorders: Theory, Research, and Treatment* 5, no. 3 (July 2014): 323–333.

Baumrind, D. 1967. "Child Care Practices Anteceding Three Patterns of Preschool Behavior." *Genetic Psychology Monographs* 75, no. 1: 43–88.

Behary, W. T. 2013. *Disarming the Narcissist: Surviving and Thriving with the Self-Absorbed*, 2nd ed. Oakland, CA: New Harbinger Publications.

Boone, M. S., J. Gregg, and L. W. Coyne. 2020. *Stop Avoiding Stuff: 25 Microskills to Face Your Fears and Do It Anyway*. Oakland, CA: New Harbinger Publications.

Boss, P. 2002. "Ambiguous Loss in Families of the Missing." *The Lancet* V, no. 360: S39–S40.

Bourne, E. J. 1995. *The Anxiety and Phobia Workbook*. Oakland, CA: New Harbinger Publications.

Brackett, M. 2019. *Permission to Feel: Unlocking the Power of Emotions to Help Our Kids, Ourselves, and Our Society Thrive.* New York: Macmillan Publishers.

Brown, B. 2007. *I Thought It Was Just Me (But It Isn't) Making the Journey from "What Will People Think?" to "I Am Enough."* New York: Avery.

Brummelman, E., S. Thomaes, S. A. Nelemans, B. O. de Castro, G. Overbeek, and B. J. Bushman. 2015. "Origins of Narcissism in Children." *Proceedings of the National Academy of Sciences* 112, no. 12: 3659–3662.

Chödrön, P. 2018. *Comfortable with Uncertainty: 108 Teachings on Cultivating Fearlessness and Compassion.* Boulder, CO: Shambhala Publications.

Daitch, C. 2018. "Cognitive Behavioral Therapy, Mindfulness, and Hypnosis as Treatment Methods for Generalized Anxiety Disorder." *The American Journal of Clinical Hypnosis* 61, no. 1: 57–69.

Dentale, F., V. Verrastro, I. Petruccelli, P. Diotaiuti, F. Petruccelli, L. Cappelli, and P. San Martini. 2015. "Relationship Between Parental Narcissism and Children's Mental Vulnerability: Mediation Role of Rearing Style." *The International Journal of Psychology and Psychological Therapy* 15, no. 3: 337–347.

Donaldson-Pressman, S., and R. M. Pressman. 1994. *The Narcissistic Family: Diagnosis and Treatment.* San Francisco, CA: Jossey-Bass.

Durvasula, R. S. 2021. *"Don't You Know Who I Am?" How to Stay Sane in an Era of Narcissism, Entitlement, and Incivility.* New York: Post Hill Press.

Ekman, P. 1999. "Basic Emotions." In *The Handbook of Cognition and Emotion,* edited by T. Dalgleish and T. Power, 45–60. Sussex, UK: John Wiley & Sons.

Evans, D. R., and S. C. Segerstrom. 2011. "Why Do Mindful People Worry Less?" *Cognitive Therapy and Research* 35, no. 6: 505–510.

Fox, D. J. 2018. *Narcissistic Personality Disorder Toolbox.* Eau Claire, WI: PESI Publishing & Media.

Golec de Zavala, A., D. Lantos, and D. Bowden. 2017. "Yoga Poses Increase Subjective Energy and State Self-Esteem in Comparison to 'Power Poses.'" *Frontiers in Psychology* 8: 752.

Goleman, D. 1995. *Emotional Intelligence.* New York: Penguin Random House.

Gordon, T., and J. Borushok. 2017. *The ACT Approach: A Comprehensive Guide to Acceptance & Commitment Therapy.* Eau Claire, WI: PESI Publishing & Media.

Gottman, J. M. 1998. *Raising an Emotionally Intelligent Child: The Heart of Parenting.* New York: Simon & Schuster.

Hammond, D. C. 1990. *Handbook of Hypnotic Suggestions and Metaphors.* New York: W. W. Norton & Company.

Harris, R. 2019. *ACT Made Simple: An Easy-to-Read Primer on Acceptance and Commitment Therapy,* 2nd ed. Oakland, CA: New Harbinger Publications.

Hart, C. M., R. D. Bush-Evans, E. G. Hepper, and H. M. Hickman. 2017. "The Children of Narcissus: Insights into Narcissists' Parenting Styles." *Personality and Individual Differences* 117: 245–254.

Hayes, S. C., K. D. Strosahl, and K. G. Wilson. 2012. *Acceptance and Commitment Therapy: The Process and Practice of Mindful Change.* New York: Guilford Press.

Hayes, S. C. 2005. *Get Out of Your Mind and Into Your Life.* Oakland, CA: New Harbinger Publications.

Hill, D., and D. Sorenson. 2021. *ACT Daily Journal: Get Unstuck and Live Fully with Acceptance and Commitment Therapy.* Oakland, CA: New Harbinger Publications.

Joseph, S. 2011. *What Doesn't Kill Us: The New Psychology of Posttraumatic Growth.* New York: Basic Books.

Kabat-Zinn, J. 1990. *Full Catastrophe Living: Using the Wisdom of Your Body to Face Stress, Pain, and Illness.* New York: Bantam Books.

Kay, K., and C. Shipman. 2014. *The Confidence Code: The Science and Art of Self-Assurance—What Women Should Know.* New York: HarperCollins.

Kertz, S. J., J. Koran, K. T. Stevens, and T. Björgvinsson. 2015. "Repetitive Negative Thinking Predicts Depression and Anxiety Symptom Improvement During Brief Cognitive Behavioral Therapy." *Behaviour Research and Therapy* 68: 54–63.

Korn, E. R., and G. J. Pratt. 1990. "Mental Rehearsal: The Protective Shield." In *Handbook of Hypnotic Suggestions and Metaphors,* edited by D. C. Hammond. New York: W.W. Norton & Company.

Lee, J. J., D. Cable, and B. Staats. 2014. "Endure and Innovate: Effects of Reflected Best Self Exercise on Resilience and Creativity." *Academy of Management Proceedings* 1: 13402.

Larimer, M. E., R. S. Palmer, and G. A. Marlatt. 1999. "Relapse Prevention: An Overview of Marlatt's Cognitive-Behavioral Model." *Alcohol Research & Health* 23, no. 2: 151–160.

Levine, M. 2012. *Teach Your Children Well: Parenting for Authentic Success.* New York: HarperCollins.

McBride, K. 2013. *Will I Ever Be Good Enough: Healing the Daughters of Narcissistic Mothers.* New York: Atria.

McCall, T. 2007. *Yoga as Medicine: The Yogic Prescription for Health and Healing.* New York: Random House.

Malkin, C. 2015. *Rethinking Narcissism: The Secret to Recognizing and Coping with Narcissism.* New York: HarperCollins.

Martin, S. 2021. *The Better Boundaries Workbook: A CBT-Based Program to Help You Set Limits, Express Your Needs, and Create Healthy Relationships.* Oakland, CA: New Harbinger Publications.

Mazza, M. T. 2020. *The ACT Workbook for OCD: Mindfulness, Acceptance, and Exposure Skills to Live Well with Obsessive-Compulsive Disorder.* Oakland, CA: New Harbinger Publications.

Mindell, P. 2001. *How to Say It for Women: Communicating with Confidence and Power Using the Language of Success.* New York: Penguin.

Monteregge, S., A. Tsagkalidou, P. Cuijpers, and P. Spinhoven. 2020. "The Effects of Different Types of Treatment for Anxiety on Repetitive

Negative Thinking: A Meta-Analysis." *Clinical Psychology: Science and Practice* 27, no. 2.

Morrow, K. J., and E. DuPont Spencer. 2018. *CBT for Anxiety: A Step-by-Step Training Manual for the Treatment of Fear, Panic, Worry, and OCD.* Eau Claire, WI: PESI Publishing & Media.

Neff, K. 2011. *Self-Compassion: Stop Beating Yourself Up and Leave Insecurity Behind.* New York: HarperCollins.

Neff, K., and C. Germer. 2018. *The Mindful Self-Compassion Workbook: A Proven Way to Accept Yourself, Build Inner Strength, and Thrive.* New York: The Guilford Press.

Neimeyer, R. A. 2021. "Conversation Starters." AfterTalk. https://www .aftertalk.com/conversation_starters.

Peterson, C., and M. E. P. Seligman. 2004. *Character Strengths and Virtues: A Handbook and Classification.* London, UK: Oxford University Press.

Pfafman, T. 2017. "Assertiveness." In *Encyclopedia of Personality and Individual Differences,* edited by V. Zeigler-Hill and T. K. Shackelford. New York: Springer International Publishing.

Porges, M. 2020. *What Girls Need: How to Raise Bold, Courageous, and Resilient Women.* New York: Penguin Random House.

Roberts, L. M., E. D. Heaphy, and B. Barker Caza. May 2019. "To Become Your Best Self, Study Your Successes." *Harvard Business Review* (May 14).

Roberts, L. M., G. Spreitzer, J. E. Dutton, R. E. Quinn, E. D. Heaphy, and B. Barker. 2005. "How to Play to Your Strengths." *Harvard Business Review* (January).

Ronningstam, E. 2017. "Intersect Between Self-Esteem and Emotion Regulation in Narcissistic Personality Disorder—Implications for Alliance Building and Treatment." *Borderline Personality Disorder and Emotion Dysregulation* 4, no. 3 (February 7).

Russ, E., J. Shedler, R. Bradley, and D. Westen. 2008. "Refining the Construct of Narcissistic Personality Disorder: Diagnostic Criteria and Subtypes." *American Journal of Psychiatry,* 165, no. 11: 1473–1481.

Seligman, M. E., T. A. Steen, N. Park, and C. Peterson. 2005. "Positive Psychology Progress: Empirical Validation of Interventions." *The American Psychologist* 60(5), 410–421.

Stinson, F. S., D. A. Dawson, R. B. Goldstein, S. P. Chou, B. Huang, S. M. Smith, W. J. Ruan, A. J. Pulay, T. D. Saha, R. P. Pickering, and B. F. Grant. 2008. "Prevalence, Correlates, Disability, and Comorbidity of DSM-IV Narcissistic Personality Disorder: Results from the Wave 2 National Epidemiologic Survey on Alcohol and Related Conditions." *The Journal of Clinical Psychiatry* 69, no. 7: 1033–1045.

Stoddard, J. A., and N. Afari. 2014. *The Big Book of ACT Metaphors: A Practitioner's Guide to Experiential Exercises & Metaphors in Acceptance and Commitment Therapy.* Oakland, CA: New Harbinger Publications.

Tedeschi, R. G., and L. G. Calhoun. 2004. "Posttraumatic Growth: Conceptual Foundations and Empirical Evidence." *Psychological Inquiry* 15, no. 1: 1–18.

US Department of Health and Human Services, Health Resources and Services Administration. 2013. *Women's Health USA 2013.* Rockville, MD: US Department of Health and Human Services.

Van Dijk, S. 2012. *Calming the Emotional Storm: Using Dialectical Behavior Therapy Skills to Manage Your Emotions and Balance Your Life.* Oakland, CA: New Harbinger Publications.

Via Institute on Character, https://www.viacharacter.org/.

Walser, R. D., and D. Westrup. 2007. *Acceptance and Commitment Therapy for the Treatment of Post-Traumatic Stress Disorder and Trauma-Related Problems: A Practitioner's Guide to Using Mindfulness and Acceptance Strategies.* Oakland CA: New Harbinger Publications.

Wolfelt, A. D. 2016. "Why Is the Funeral Ritual Important?" Center for Loss and Life Transition. https://www.centerforloss.com/2016/12 /funeral-ritual-important.

Stephanie M. Kriesberg, PsyD, has practiced clinical psychology for twenty-five years. A graduate of the Ferkauf Graduate School of Psychology of Yeshiva University, she is trained in psychodynamic psychotherapy, cognitive behavioral therapy (CBT), and acceptance and commitment therapy (ACT). In addition, she is trained in the practice of clinical hypnosis. Kriesberg is on the board of the New England Society of Clinical Hypnosis.

Foreword writer Wendy Terrie Behary, LCSW, is founder and clinical director of The Cognitive Therapy Center of New Jersey, and codirector of The Schema Therapy Institutes of NJ-NYC-DC. She is author of *Disarming the Narcissist*.

Real change *is* possible

For more than forty-five years, New Harbinger has published proven-effective self-help books and pioneering workbooks to help readers of all ages and backgrounds improve mental health and well-being, and achieve lasting personal growth. In addition, our spirituality books offer profound guidance for deepening awareness and cultivating healing, self-discovery, and fulfillment.

Founded by psychologist Matthew McKay and Patrick Fanning, New Harbinger is proud to be an independent, employee-owned company. Our books reflect our core values of integrity, innovation, commitment, sustainability, compassion, and trust. Written by leaders in the field and recommended by therapists worldwide, New Harbinger books are practical, accessible, and provide real tools for real change.

 **newharbinger**publications

MORE BOOKS from
NEW HARBINGER PUBLICATIONS

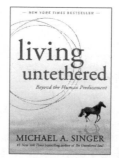
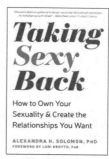

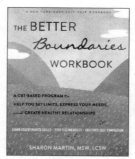

Did you know there are **free tools** you can download for this book?

Free tools are things like **worksheets, guided meditation exercises,** and **more** that will help you get the most out of your book.

You can download free tools for this book— whether you bought or borrowed it, in any format, from any source—from the New Harbinger website. All you need is a NewHarbinger.com account. Just use the URL provided in this book to view the free tools that are available for it. Then, click on the "download" button for the free tool you want, and follow the prompts that appear to log in to your NewHarbinger.com account and download the material.

You can also save the free tools for this book to your **Free Tools Library** so you can access them again anytime, just by logging in to your account! Just look for this button on the book's free tools page.

+ Save this to my free tools library

If you need help accessing or downloading free tools, visit **newharbinger.com/faq** or contact us at **customerservice@newharbinger.com**.